Praise for *Make Lemonade*

"Alicia brilliantly identifies divorce as a portal for personal transformation. This masterpiece provides an empowering road map to not only get *through* your divorce, but to transform your darkest days into a powerful catalyst to become the highest version of yourself. Alicia boldly leads by example and shows you how to create a "next chapter" that will, undoubtedly, exceed your deepest desires—all delivered in a truly practical, child-focused, and compassionate way."

RADHIKA LAKHANI, Divorce Lawyer, Mediator & Conscious Co-Parenting Coach

"Whether the end of your marriage left you with a couple of bruised lemons or a big bag of rotten ones, this book will guide you to do exactly what its title promises: make lemonade. With wisdom and insight from her own journey, plus delightful spice and wit, Alicia Robertson offers compassion, action, and most of all companionship for your journey through and after divorce."

SHANNON MORONEY, MA RSW, Therapist & Bestselling Author of *Through the Glass* and *Heal for Real*

MAKE
LEMONADE

Thrive Through Divorce by Transforming Your Life

MAKE LEMONADE

ALICIA ROBERTSON

PAGE TWO

For Ava and Giacomo, who are my reason.

This book is not intended as a substitute for professional psychotherapy or counselling. The reader should regularly consult with a professional in matters relating to emotional, mental, and physical well-being. The intention of the author is to support planning, accountability, and growth through separation and divorce, but the author is not a licensed therapist or counsellor.

Cataloguing in publication information is available from Library and Archives Canada.
ISBN 978-1-77458-208-4 (paperback)
ISBN 978-1-77458-209-1 (ebook)

The film quote on page 64 is from *The Holiday* (2006), written and directed by Nancy Meyer, presented by Columbia Pictures and Universal Pictures, and produced by Waverly Films in association with Relativity Media.

The contents of this book are a mix of personal experiences and the stories and perspectives of the author's clients. Some names and details have been changed to protect anonymity.

Page Two
pagetwo.com

Edited by Cristen Iris and Amanda Lewis
Cover and interior design by Taysia Louie
Cover photo by Darius Bashar
Interior illustrations by Lab Creative

lemonadelife.ca

"When life is sweet, say thank you
and celebrate. And when life
is bitter, say thank you and grow."

SHAUNA NIEQUIST

Contents

Introduction
About This Girl

I N AUGUST 2015, just six weeks after delivering our second child, I looked into my husband's eyes and knew that my marriage was over. I wouldn't accept it for many more months, but in that moment, I knew.

The thing is, the moment that changes a life is never about that one moment. It's about a million past moments and a million future moments.

As a sensitive optimist, hopeless romantic, and fantastical dreamer, I believe in fairy tales and happy endings. I approached my life with this sense of naïveté, blissfully overlooking the telltale signs that warned me to make changes. I avoided conflict and uncomfortable truths, an indirect resistance to seeing the many signs of our marriage degrading over the years.

Years before the *It's over* moment my husband and I shared, a friend and I sat musing about our marriages. We wondered if we could improve them by going to therapy. We admitted to each other, in a raw and vulnerable moment, that if we did go for counselling there would be no turning back—we might find problems we didn't know existed or would not have the strength or will to change. Better to keep Pandora's box firmly sealed than to find out we could do better in our marriages.

I decided I was willing to settle and compromise in the hope that I could keep it together for as long as possible— because marriage is for life regardless of any unhappiness or dysfunction, right?

What I know now is that when we don't have the courage to open that box, we become stuck in fear and discomfort, feelings that will certainly become a marriage-ending problem. If we don't examine the problem, we can endure soul-sucking loneliness in our marriages.

There's a limit to how long we can avoid the tough stuff, the real conversations. But, for some time, I blamed our problems on anything I could. I used clichés to justify my lack of attention and action. I told myself:

This too shall pass.

Marriage is tough in the beginning as you start to knit your life together.

Every relationship needs work.

With little money, experience, or status, my husband Lee and I had achieved the beautiful home, the white picket fence, and the million-dollar careers. Then the trials and tribulations of starting a new family complicated our already busy lives and struggling relationship. I figured that too would pass. I became skilled at covering my stress, anxiety, and loneliness with fun, hustle, and bustle. I threw myself into the excitement of building a business, travelling, socializing, and the work-hard, play-hard lifestyle. And all the while my connection to my husband weakened.

Downtime literally meant sleeping. I believed that as long as we were aligned in the frequency of our desire for sex, everything was fine. I comforted myself with reassurances

If we don't examine the problem, **we can endure soul-sucking loneliness in our marriages.**

from friends that infrequent physical intimacy is to be expected in marriage.

As time passed, we lived a fabulous life with few worries about money, health, friends, family, home, or business. We had all the success boxes checked and frankly could have had anything we wanted. I thought, *Who am I to feel unhappy or unfulfilled?* I thought that maybe I was just an unhappy person, and if all of this couldn't make me happy, perhaps nothing would. So what would be the point of starting over? And, in truth, part of me loved all the hype and our flashy, lavish lifestyle. It was a total rush.

But then I remembered that what had once made me happy were the simple pleasures of outdoor adventures, summers spent camping, stolen moments without purpose, drop-bys and random conversations about nothing. These weren't happening anymore, or at least not as often.

I thought I could have it all, but I discovered early on that the lifestyle we shared did not match my true needs and desires. I suppose I thought he or I would change, but the more I lived in his vision of the ideal life, the further I drifted from my authentic self. Without those quiet times and simple pleasures, I began to experience a deep sense of loss.

I started to wonder what the heck we would do together when we were older and the distractions of youth and striving ebbed away. But, at that point, I don't think either of us understood that the gap was wide as it was. The moment I realized that something was terribly off—that there was no fixing my marriage, and that I wasn't going to get the fairy-tale ending I'd imagined—it came as quite a shock.

I went through all the stages of grief, starting with denial and bargaining. I prayed so hard every night that God would give my husband back to me and that our family would be saved. Deep down I knew my prayers wouldn't be answered.

I knew that divorce was my fate and that I was meant to live a different life, but I could not yet untangle my co-dependence, shame, and guilt. Had I been given the option, I would have sold my soul to keep it all together.

After holding out for just over a year, unwilling to give him the exit he craved, I finally let go. Something had to give, or all the stress and anxiety and walking on eggshells would make us desperately ill.

During those months something inside me rose, and I felt an undeniable shift toward my potential. I was devastated, but I learned a lot about myself and how to recognize that potential and the possibilities life has to offer.

I learned how to thrive through my divorce with grit and grace, and to hold my head high. I learned how to transform my life and officially show up as the author of my own story. Because I am no sidekick; I am the motherfucking leading lady!

I knew it was time to become whole, hopeful, and happy again.

This book is about how to strategically play nice in the sandbox. My hope is that it allows you to follow a similar arc: from vulnerable to your wild, powerful self.

What to Expect

The flow of this book follows my own journey, but I intentionally designed it to be used in multiple ways. This is very much a "choose your own adventure" thing, because each of us experiences different things at different times. Some of you may be co-habitating during your separation like I did, and some may have already been long separated from your spouse. Others will find yourselves divorced and juggling many new situations in rapid succession or all at once. So

*I'm not going to lie
and say it's not
hard, because it is.*
**But the payoff
is huge.**

maybe you want to read page by page, or maybe you want to jump around. Do what works for you.

This is not a book about how to get the most out of a divorce settlement or how to win at divorce. It's about how to build a life through and beyond divorce. This book will teach you how to model greatness. But to do that, you've gotta grow. Because you can't create something new by using the same energy that got you to this place.

Part I is for those who are still in shock. This is the real and raw stuff that you're dealing with every second of every day, the stuff that's so heavy it pins you to the sofa. This part covers the period between discovering that your marriage and wife identity are over to when you begin to understand your authentic self, knowing who you are and what you want. You will learn to give yourself time to grieve and to solidify your values, and how to be unattached.

I was in this phase for two years. I could only handle so much in the first year amidst denial, bargaining, sadness, and anger. By the second year, I had accepted the end of our relationship, and that allowed me to continue my progress by conquering new things, as well as things that felt new again. To be clear, I was still sad and angry. But at that point, I understood why I was feeling that way, and I started to carve out a regular practice for processing, healing, and letting go.

By the end of this leg of your journey, you will have processed the most painful and debilitating emotions and will be on your way to establishing a peaceful and productive ongoing partnership with your former partner (or at least to operating in a healthy way on your side of things).

Part II of this book is about finding your new normal and practicing the art of walking in your own power. This phase is about ownership, learning, and managing change. It's a time when you have figured out who you are, what you want, and how you'll interact with your former partner if you'll be co-parenting.

You'll have established new routines and rituals that bring continuity to your flow. This is an opportunity to settle into and enjoy those rituals, and add what you need more of and subtract whatever is not working. This is a time of continued healing and progress. Now that you have some big wins and new lifestyle habits to count on, you can start having fun and layer on new things.

You will begin to see the blessings of the silver lining that is life after divorce. You'll be ready to dream. You'll be able to see yourself in a better place, a place of your own creation.

Okay. I know what you're thinking. You're thinking that this sounds hard, like it's going to put you right back into traumas and dramas. I'm not going to lie and say it's not hard, because it is. But the payoff is *huge*.

Part III is where this path opens to spectacular vistas and intersects with myriad options. Things start to get good. I mean *really* good, because you'll have reconnected with who you are, established boundaries, and be consistently living out your core values. These new patterns will allow you to aspire to new goals and dare to be vulnerable again. You'll be taking on a lot of firsts.

You living your best life means sharing the best of life with other people. That can be scary after the hurt of sharing life with someone only to be rejected, but that hurt is just a reminder that the person who rejected you had a purpose in your life, and that purpose is over. You'll have the space and emotional bandwidth to find your people. And if not now, when? You'll be well equipped even if it's still scary. You'll also be craving the company of supportive, like-minded people. Finding your inner circle will give you the opportunity to use the wisdom and perspective you've gained and the transformation you've gone through to begin to establish a legacy that will make a difference for you, your family, and the world at large.

The Path Begins Here

No matter how difficult it may seem right now, it's time to take your first step. Don't worry. I've walked this road before, and I've crumpled. My tears have soaked the rocks along the way. My sobs have drowned out the sound of singing birds. But the only way to the other side is through. I made it. So can you. I'll be with you every step of the way, and I promise that you'll feel the warmth of the sun on your face and hear the birds sing again.

Divorce is a catalyst for change, prompting us to face our fears and commit to being our best version, whether we're in a relationship or single. We owe it to ourselves and everyone around us to be the best version of ourselves that we can be, even if that means walking away from or letting go of marriage so we can achieve personal greatness.

Deciding to end your relationship may feel almost impossible. The lack of control you feel if your spouse decides it's over may feel even worse. I guarantee that it *is* possible, and it *will* get better. You *can* do this. Take my hand, and let's go.

one

·······

DROP
THE
FEAR

1

· · · · ·

Face the Unknown

MY CAREFULLY built world crumbled on a hot summer day as I stood on the threshold of our home gym room where my husband, Lee, was working out. The signs that something was very wrong had become too big for me to ignore. I mustered my courage and spoke into the void: "Should I be worried about our marriage?"

He immediately sat down. He didn't even look at me. My heart sank. He put his head between his hands. My heart sank further, and my full brain wished that he would look up at me like he used to and assure me that it was going to be all right and that we were going through a rough patch. I'd just given birth after struggling through a difficult pregnancy, something that would strain any relationship. With our house, white picket fence, and two kids—one girl and one boy—everything was going to plan. At least that's what it looked like from the outside. I figured that the other stuff would shake out in time.

Lee was good at solving our problems. He was my rock. But he didn't look like a rock at that moment. Several long seconds later, he raised his head and said, "I don't know."

I heard his words. They were painful but the words, that open-ended answer, gave me hope. But it was the look in his eyes—and knowing him better than he knew himself—that told me what I didn't want to hear. He was gone. He no longer wanted to be married to me. He just didn't know how to leave because he didn't want to let me down. He had made promises he couldn't keep. He had a young family that he didn't want to break up, but he was desperate for change.

My body, my compassion and love, and the logical side of my brain all wanted to let him off the hook, to let him go right there in that very moment, because part of me knew we had legitimately come to this. It was our truth and we had to face it. But my emotions were stuck in shame and guilt and fear. I desperately wanted to control the situation. I wanted to hold on tighter and hate him and blame him and force him to realize that the promises he made needed to be fulfilled.

I couldn't accept that all of that was gone. So, I chalked it up to something Lee must be going through: a mental health issue, a midlife crisis, a full-on panic attack. If he could go away to refuel or get help or be medicated, then he'd find his way back to us and to me.

After taking time to process—and by process I mean days in bed, waves of lying on the floor in the fetal position bawling my eyes out, thoughts of suicide, catastrophizing—I called a friend who I knew would talk straight and keep what I said confidential. She was my best hope to move forward.

Putting my reality out into the world for the first time was a huge risk. Running a successful business in a small town means the personal is always public and subject to scrutiny and judgement. My husband and I were considered the gold standard of success. I had done everything "right." I graduated all the levels, worked all the jobs, earned my keep, married the man of my dreams, built a life and a business—a million-dollar family for the win! I was living the dream, right?

Wrong! When I realized my marriage was ending, it challenged my entire identity. Sharing my new reality and my desperate need made me feel like a fraud. I was in uncharted territory, and I was terrified.

Identify Your Fears

My worst fears were coming true—failing, falling out of people's good graces, not being seen as perfect. I presumed judgement and felt shame. In the days, weeks, and even months after I realized that Lee was there but not present, I allowed my fears of starting over and of what others would think to fuel a self-sabotaging machine. I was so afraid of being alone that I convinced myself to convince him to stay.

I can do more to make him happy, I thought. *I can help him solve whatever issues he is having.* But these beliefs simply reduced me further, because my whole identity was wrapped up in one word: *wife*. The thought of failing, losing, and being fired from the role of Mrs. So and So seemed an unbearable burden. No matter what I offered or what I did, it was clear. Lee had no desire to work on the marriage any longer—he may have been confused about how to move forward, but he was done.

Despite knowing this, I still thought I had a fighting chance to do the work and create the changes I wanted to see. I'm laughing out loud and shaking my head as I write this, but that really is what I thought. And I worked damn hard at it for an entire year. During that year of limbo and denial, I slowly started to see, and then face, my co-dependence, shame, and guilt.

We slept in separate beds. We no longer shared intimate spaces like dressing areas, no longer went to social events together. When Lee was home, he interacted only with the children. I was so goddamn envious of our little children that they would be able to have their father forever while I was losing him.

When Lee moved out and we started to share custody, I was devastated and reeling. I didn't know who I was or what to do with my time. My children were very young, and my activity was tied to two things: the business I'd helped Lee build and being a mom. Mom was my primary role and where the largest share of my self-worth came from. Many of us give up everything to be moms. And suddenly this role we're super proud of is taken away. Or so we think in our darkest times, as if mother is somehow inseparable from wife.

I was afraid of the possibility that my children wouldn't need me and weren't going to be under my watchful eye. I thought they might someday have an entirely different family and their lives would move on without me. My dream family was suddenly this separate thing, and I wasn't part of the picture. I did my darndest to stay in that family portrait.

Slowly, sometimes ever so slowly, I started to understand that divorce and co-parenting were my reality and there was no changing it. *The Four Agreements* by Don Miguel Ruiz helped me navigate the bargaining and denial stages. It helped me stick to facts, not take things personally, and do my best; it helped get my head out of what-if scenarios and my heart out of fantasies of reconciliation. I realized I could be in control of my situation, or at least of many aspects of it.

Suddenly I could see that while my situation was not my choice, it had both everything and nothing to do with me. I recognized that what Lee was telling me was the truth. I couldn't believe my own story, or anybody else's who would tell me that he and I were just going through a difficult time and that it would pass.

It's true what they say: When somebody shows themselves to you, believe it. So if I caught myself denying or

Win the tiny battles, then slowly engage in the **bigger battles and earn bigger wins.**

bargaining, I would remind myself of the truth I heard in Lee's words, felt in his energy, and saw in his eyes. Our marriage was over.

Understand Your Fears

When divorce is the only option, it means that one or both people are so unhappy that the most painful choice is the only choice for survival. If you're like I was at that time in my life, you're afraid of being afraid. You're stuck in that fear mode, and it's debilitating. You may not even be allowing yourself to process how scary these things are, for fear of knowing what you must face in the days and weeks to come. Or you might be looking backward, terrified that your past failures will overtake and devour you.

One thing's for sure: If we don't face our fears, adopt a growth mindset, and accept our own our shit, we'll stay stuck. Yes, we may move on to a new relationship, but we won't actually overcome anything or grow wiser. I think that's why second marriages have an even higher failure rate than first marriages—because people haven't looked their fears in the face, shoved them aside, and stepped beyond them.

About a year after hearing Lee speak the words "I don't know" while his body screamed *I'm out*, I put my feelings into words.

I feared chaos, so I tried to control everything.

I feared emptiness, so I stayed busy.

I feared even the whiff of failure, so I always showed up oozing with enthusiasm.

I feared being undefinable, so I identified as a wife and mother.

I feared a future that wouldn't match the one I'd worked so hard to create.

But as I looked at these things and admitted them to myself, I felt a shift. I realized that I didn't need to be afraid of failure. I didn't need to fear the future. What I did need was to take responsibility for living at half capacity, for not showing up one hundred percent in my life, and for not being honest about where I was and what was going on.

The funny thing is that I'm a Type A. Many of the women I now coach through their divorces are Type As. We love control, and we hate chaos. Chaos causes floods of negative emotions. Being in control of a situation brings us a level of calm. It's how we self-soothe.

One of the most humbling things about my experience has been the realization that my need to control everything was leading me to get results in an inauthentic way. I was checking all the boxes and appeared to be in control, but I wasn't actually in control because the only way for us to truly take control is to acknowledge our inefficiencies, ineffectiveness, and weaknesses, and to learn to appreciate that all these things build character. Nobody is great at everything. There's no way to talk about strengths without talking about weaknesses or to appreciate wins without feeling losses. It's important to see things for what they are and to celebrate the truly beautiful qualities that we possess, which we can use to tame the out-of-control aspects of our lives.

Easier said than done though, right?

The most prominent narratives out there for women in out-of-control situations are the martyr, the victim, the drama queen, and the scorned woman. Those tropes don't help one single bit, and, at worst, they can feed our fears. I needed to find ways to take control through a positive process. No avoidance, no manipulation, no drama, no nonsense. Just me, myself, and I figuring out who I am and then living in that truth.

There's no way to talk about strengths without talking about weaknesses or **to appreciate wins without feeling losses.**

Note that I'm not saying I overcame my fears, nor am I telling you to overcome yours. At the beginning, middle, and end of every day, we are always experiencing the world through our lizard brain. If you're a human, you're gonna be afraid of stuff. Lots of stuff. We just need to analyze those fears and figure out what options we have other than fight or flight. And, even then, it's not like the sadness magically goes away or we suddenly know exactly what we need to do next.

Choose to Model Greatness

I have fallen to my knees many times with pain, sorrow, and despair. I've lain in a puddle of grief on the floor, wishing I could disappear. I thought about ending my life. I'm not sure what I expected when I hit the floor. Maybe I expected relief. Expectations are a damned thing. When you hit your knees and get nothing. When your body hits the floor and you still feel nothing. How *does* the body keep running when it's gutted? In those moments, my only option was to stand up again.

I'd love to say that I did it for my own sake, but in the beginning I only got up for someone or something else: my kids, the doorbell, must-attend appointments, the appearance of normalcy. Each time I thought it was my rock bottom. Turns out it was not. Rock bottom is when you choose to rise from your knees for *yourself*.

When I was starting to figure this out, I asked Lee, "What inspires you? What are your values? What if all this business went away tomorrow—what would you do? What brings you joy?"

He was the one who'd realized he wanted out of our marriage, that it wasn't a good fit for him. I assumed he'd know what the right fit was. I thought he'd be able to answer my questions, the questions I was just now thinking to ask myself.

But he just stared at me. I was overcome by compassion for him in that moment. He was as lost as I was.

That's when I realized that by calling it quits on our marriage, he had in some twisted turn of fate given me a great gift. He had handed me my freedom. I realized we were both suffering, mentally and physically. It was a pivotal moment. Whether you are the one who calls the end of your marriage or not, you are both navigating your own personal journey with your own lessons to learn—we must transform or live in peril.

So I turned to my journal and to meditation, and I took the first step on a path to forgive him. But I realized very quickly that I had nothing to forgive him for. The forgiveness I needed was for myself, because nobody made me do anything. Nobody pushed me to this point. I made choices. I got here my own damn self, and nobody was going to get me out but me.

Learning to be compassionate to myself allowed me to take control of what I could control, or at least what I could influence. I took responsibility for myself, for my choices, and for how I think. It's as if compassion was an eyewash that helped me see clearly: I realized that, just as I needed to own my stuff, the only person who could help my former partner was himself. His stuff was his stuff.

On the other side of this divorce thing, I work with many women who are getting out of relationships with narcissistic partners and even physically abusive partners. One thing I can't underscore enough is that having compassion for someone and even forgiving them doesn't mean you're saying their behaviour is okay. Compassion doesn't wipe the slate clean. Compassion just helps us see things for what they are and get some distance from the pain so that we can seek healing.

Some people never change. That's just a fact. This isn't about them. It's about us. The truth is that good people can do bad things. It's not personal; it's just a choice that seldom has anything to do with us, and we don't have any control over it. And that's a truth that cuts both ways. Even happy, good people can hurt other people without meaning to.

Something in us was attracted to what the other person had put on the table. If we don't take a hard look at that and unpack why we made that choice, we're going to end up with that person, or a person like that, again. Compassion is about us. This journey is about the changes we want for ourselves regardless of whether our soon-to-be former partner changes a single thing in their life.

What about the Children?

For those of us who have children with the person we're divorcing, the reality is that we're probably going to have to interact with that person for a long time. The question becomes: How are we going to do this in a way that doesn't destroy or activate us every time?

The answer is to set boundaries and to understand what we can control and what we can't. And one of the most important things at this stage is to understand that this is our children's journey too. They didn't ask for this. The divorce journey is an opportunity to model greatness, to establish ourselves as leaders by setting the example of healthy, productive behaviour. But we must choose to do so before we can actually act in accordance with our choice for others—especially our children—to see.

We can't carry our children's pain. We can't remove all the inconveniences. And we can't tell them how to think and act. (Well, we can *tell* them, but we don't have any control over whether they listen.) What we can do is model greatness and teach them how to be effective communicators. We can show them what resilience looks like and how to develop coping strategies—how to be flexible and open-minded and so on. We can show them what it takes to play the long game and what it takes to lay a foundation for future success.

Some people say that during a divorce parents should focus on the kids. I look at it differently. Focusing on my journey with a goal of modelling greatness for my kids was the only way I could rise above. So, every day, I aspired to focus on myself and make great choices. That, I believe, is the best gift we can give our children.

Before I chose to find my authentic self and model greatness, the example I set for my kids was to always put other people's needs in front of our own. My behaviour said that it's okay to be a doormat. It's okay to avoid living your best life, because to do so makes some people uncomfortable and opens you up to verbal criticism.

To achieve any level of greatness, I had to stay focused on myself and the things I could control. At that time and in that space, we set goals for what was important to us as co-parents. We wanted our children to be independent, resourceful, capable, confident humans who act with kindness and respect. We had to understand and accept that how we got there—tries, near misses, fails, and wins—was going to look different in each of our homes.

Do What You Can

In the early days, I didn't always hold myself accountable for living up to my own standards or acting on facts. I justified my actions and thoughts with this reason or that excuse. But in honest moments, I knew what I needed to do—I just didn't want to do it. I needed to get my adult shit together!

Some people never change. That's just a fact. This isn't about them. **It's about us.**

Listening to our inner guide can be scary, especially when it is not in sync with our reality. Acting on it is even scarier, because it's unfamiliar and uncomfortable. I worked in business with my ex. I knew in my heart it was time to exit the business, but I was comfortable and afraid.

The key was shifting from a victim to a proactive mode. My goals were simple.

I learned to do the next thing I knew I needed to do.

Your goals should be simple too, at least in the beginning. You may have to fight to get through your divorce negotiations and separation period. This is about feeling the sense of accomplishment that comes with simply moving forward, remembering to breathe, and putting one foot in front of other.

During this time, it's critical to remember that one decision today does not have to be the decision for tomorrow or forever. You are making the most informed decisions that you can make for yourself today. When the information changes, so does the plan. The big learning opportunities are self-worth, independence, co-parenting, and new family dynamics as a single parent.

This is about understanding that, with a fresh start, nothing will be perfect.

This is about flexibility, grey areas, creativity, and being open to a lot of learning and self-expression.

Remember that you're going from partnership to single life. You're unpacking all the emotional, psychological, and physiological responses to patterns you're used to living but that are incompatible with who you really are and where you really want to go. Unpacking and undoing these things takes time and energy. This is about all the tries and fails, the try agains, the awkward moments, the sad moments, and pushing through these moments when you're running on fumes.

This is about celebrating small wins and conquering tough days. Pat yourself on the back for getting out of bed. For eating at all. Choosing not to distract yourself with vices like smoking, booze, and coffee. Not forgetting your kids at school kinda days. If getting out of bed is your only win today, good for you.

Focusing on doing just what you can do at any given moment and not judging yourself for not living up to some arbitrary ideal will, over time, carve a new groove in your mind and body. Celebrating small wins will give you energy and move you forward faster than if you try to do it by brute force, because taking small, slow steps is sustainable. It establishes a mindset of progress and self-worth.

Recently, a client said to me, "I just don't want to deal with all the demons. I just want this to go away."

My reply was simple but compassionate: "Well, you have to because it won't."

Change may feel impossible to you in this moment. Our brains fight to avoid rewiring. They signal pain and rationalize staying in the patterns we know. So, start with small, uncomfortable steps. Win the tiny battles, then slowly engage in the bigger battles and earn bigger wins.

Hey, you're reading this book, and you've kept reading even though you're pissed and gutted and I've asked you to face your fears and model greatness despite all that. That's a win!

You might not feel ready to do much else. I get it. It's okay. Consider reaching out to a friend you can trust, someone who'll keep your secrets safe and help you move through your pain.

Truth and Ownership

Before moving on together, I think it's important I tell you that the most humane thing any of us can do for someone is to speak truth. When we speak truth and when others speak truth to us, we know where we stand and are in a better position to deal with it. We humans hate uncertainty, but as shitty as a break-up is, at least we know that we need to find a new path. It motivates us—with a carrot or a stick—to take control.

This is the ownership piece: Yes, you might have been blindsided. And yes, dishonourable things may have happened. But it takes two people to end a relationship. Nothing good implodes.

Somewhere along the way to the perfect life, I lost myself doing all the "right" things. Somewhere in the back of my mind I knew that my limiting beliefs weren't serving me (or my kids). But it took years of self-discovery for me to find out who I really am and genuinely feel and accept the truth of my new reality.

When you let go of what's holding you back and keeping you down, you'll see that there is no right or wrong way to get through the end of a relationship. All of us are just living, learning, and figuring it out as we go.

2

. . . . .

Find Your
Authentic Self

WHEN I was twenty-four years old, I moved from my parents' house to my husband's house. During our marriage, I lived to make my husband happy and our family whole. I lived to make his dreams come true, so much so that I could no longer make decisions for myself. I had difficulty identifying with my own feelings because I was hyper aware of his. I adapted my mood and managed situations depending on what I believed to be his needs. It was like I was taking the temperature every evening when he'd come home. I didn't think I could communicate my needs and have them met unless I manipulated him.

His dreams became my dreams. I lived for his love. To receive his love, there was so much of me I could not be. But who was I to complain? I mean, we had a great life, or so it seemed. I slowly lost trust in my abilities, and my self-worth tanked because I valued his approval more than I valued my approval of myself.

I also substituted busy for living. Busy is not a superpower! In fact, it's easier to be busy than to deeply connect with life and all its shortcomings. Busy and stress were my world. The busier I got and the more I did, the more I was praised.

Slowly but surely in the chaos of my life, I lost sight of who I was. I couldn't tell you what my values were. I couldn't tell you what I wanted out of my life aside from the things I thought I had.

When I lost my partner, I was forced to stop running. I had to drop the act and find myself, one experience at a time. Now I understand the blessing of losing myself to find myself. Burnt-out workaholic, failing mom, wife, and friend… doing everything but nothing all at the same time.

As I started to accept my new reality, I began thinking about who I was and who I wanted to be. The word *authentic* kept popping up. I struggled with it many times. I wondered, What is this word *authenticity*? I searched the term on Google again and again, but each search result only led me to deeper questions. What does "authentic self" mean? What is this? What am I doing? When you've allowed yourself to be absorbed into another person's sense of self, you can't even conceive of how to be anything different.

Then it dawned on me. I needed to ask different questions, questions Google can't answer. My questions became different. How do I find out who I am? What is it that I enjoy? Do I enjoy tennis lessons, Zumba classes, walking in nature? Do I enjoy team or independent activities, small class sizes or large? Do I like cooking, baking, hosting, or ordering takeout? What do I have to share with the world? What do I want to share? I didn't know the answer to any of these things.

At some point, I came to the realization that authenticity is when our intentions or goals are aligned with our values.

Our values are our code of conduct, our moral compass. Values determine how we make decisions every day. A list of core values opens the door to possibilities and closes the door on things we know to be detrimental to us or things we're simply not interested in.

This is critical, because if we don't know what our values are, it's really hard to make good decisions when we're under pressure. And so many of the decisions we're forced to make as we go through separation and divorce have short-, medium-, and long-term effects.

A big part of this process is taking off the masks we put on for others. Our masks are the things we do and the way we talk that lead people to think that we're somebody we're not. The longer we wear our masks, the harder it is for us to separate ourselves from the character they represent, and for others to change their perception of us.

As you move through this process, especially during a divorce and especially if you're upward of forty, some people will dismiss your process as a midlife crisis. If you've already started questioning who you are as an individual, you might be thinking that's what this is. It isn't. It's you stepping into your Self. You're evolving and getting comfortable with life as it is and who you are in it. Your midlife transformation is ongoing and ever evolving.

Connect with Your Core Values

Upon further reflection, I'm not sure that I ever met my authentic self. As a sensitive, empathetic people pleaser, I always morphed to meet other people's expectations. I always dreamed of more but understood that I had to follow the rules if I wanted to be liked by everyone.

And I was right. My authentic self is not liked by everyone, but as I discovered my authentic self, a Self grounded in *my* values, hopes, and dreams, I began to effortlessly attract others with similar values and visions and repel those who don't overlap with who I really am. If that's rejection, I'll take it!

So what are values, exactly? Values are the fundamental beliefs that guide or motivate our actions. They give us purpose, a reason to exist and do what we do. Success is when our purpose matches our values. And then a funny thing happens... happiness!

Whether we realize it or not, we all have values. We just might not have labelled them yet. We might not be consciously aware of our values until something happens and we have a reaction that feels uncomfortable, or we are filled with resentment and contempt. Simply put, when we feel like we have lost ourselves or when we no longer recognize the face in the mirror, that's usually a sign that we've been living according to other people's values. It most certainly means that the boundaries we need to protect our code of conduct have failed.

It might be scary to lean into the discomfort of putting yourself first or trusting your intuition after years of self-sacrifice and ignoring your heart. But it's so important to understand who you are and what you want if you are going to live in alignment and match your actions with your values.

Here are some of the things other women and I have thought about as we leaned in with curiosity about who we are and what we value:

- How do I want to feel?
- What makes me feel safe?
- What/who am I grateful for?
- What/who/where energizes me?
- What/who/where depletes me?
- How do I rest?
- How do I play and have leisure?

*The longer we wear
our masks, the
harder it is for us to*
**separate ourselves
from the character
they represent.**

- What serves my highest self?
- What makes me feel good?
- What depletes my energy?
- Do I prefer active or passive activities?
- How do I like to have connection and intimacy?
- How do I communicate my feelings, needs, and desires?
- What conflict-resolution tactics do I like and not like?
- What is my intention for my future?
- Do I prefer flexibility or structure?
- Am I a city mouse or a country mouse?
- Am I a house person or a loft gal?
- What types of vacations do I prefer?
- What level of income and savings makes me feel financially secure?
- How do I like to spend money?
- How do I like to spend my time: by myself or with others?

When we know what our values are, we can prioritize them and develop plans in any given situation. Our values determine what we show up to in life and what we do once we're there. This will become more obvious as you move through the rest of this book. For now, just be aware that this is a good time to learn and practice mindfulness as a way to build the mental resilience you need to uncover your truth. Challenge that inner dialogue, those reactions and thoughts, so that you can get out of fear, ego, and limiting beliefs and into your true heart's desire.

During this process, it's also important to see yourself clearly. Set aside your fear and judgement when you look in the mirror and see things about yourself that aren't ideal. You don't have to be your aspirational self on every level. You've got to choose your battles at this point. One of the greatest gifts I gave myself was permission to be my entire

Self, which means honouring all of my weaknesses, short-coming, craziness, whatever those things are, because they're part of me.

I mean really, some things just aren't that important. Perfection is not the goal. In fact, striving for perfection (whatever the hell that is) is how a lot of us lost ourselves in the first place. Doing the same thing won't get you through this. Besides, finding yourself is a life-long journey. You're not just going to be able to simply read this book or go on a meditation retreat and check a box. Give yourself time and space while also taking those tiny steps—getting out of bed, making yourself a sandwich, playing a game with your kids—that will get you to the small wins you need so much at this stage. A sense of authenticity will emerge.

Authentic Self versus Personality Traits

I've come to appreciate that values define us and serve as boundaries and tools of self-discovery. When Lee and I were separated but living together, there were days when I thought, *I just don't give a shit right now. I'm just going to be gluttonous.* I started binge drinking. I was a "glass of wine with dinner every night" kind of gal. I thought that having booze around was normal and that everybody drank every night. That modelling skewed my perspective and made it easier for me to justify using alcohol to numb my pain. At the same time, I realized this was not healthy.

So, I developed a plan. I limited my drinking. In some situations, I wouldn't drink at all. When I wanted a drink, I reminded myself of what I valued—being in control of my emotions and mental faculties.

Once I defined that value and took small, doable steps to align myself with it, I got closer to my authentic self. I

You don't have to be your aspirational self on every level. **You've got to choose your battles.**

realized that I'm not an all-or-nothing person. I value moderation. So now, if I can do it from a healthy emotional and physical space, I'll have that drink. I'll eat those cookies or that extra piece of chocolate or whatever and celebrate what it means to me instead of using it as a means of escape.

No discussion about values and authenticity would be complete without at least mentioning personality. In my work with women in the throes of unwifing, I often talk about personality types and how they play into our core values and authentic self.

The important thing to remember is that our core values rarely change. Like personality, they're set. As we mature, we begin to express different aspects of our personality. We evolve into a better version of ourselves. And as we do, we're able to get closer and closer to the "real" part of who we are. When it comes to our personality, I think it would be fair to say that our potential is infinite because we're all born of love. And our personalities are what they are because the world needs us.

The downside of being hyper aware of personality typing is that the lists of traits are made by someone else. It's a pseudo-science that has utility but isn't concrete. If we focus too much on it, we start to let other people label us. We can start to feel judged and shamed and boxed in again. We start limiting ourselves, which is the thing we're trying to overcome in this moment.

So, who do you want to be? What do you, apart from everyone else, value on a moral level? And what do you enjoy? And what do you need at this exact point in your life?

It might seem like finding your values, and all this talk of authentic self and modelling, is almost an academic affair, a pure logic thing. It isn't. Feelings can betray us, and they can be a powerful guide. One of the things I've found is that it's just as helpful to let how you feel guide you. Ask yourself this powerful question: How do I want to feel?

Do you want to feel healthy, strong, empowered? Great. Now ask yourself this: What activities—that are reasonable for me to do right now—give me those good vibes?

Smoking and drinking and the suffering of hangovers at first seemed like a better alternative than waking up fully aware of the pain of my life. It was an *Oh, this sucks, but I don't have to focus on the other thing that sucks* approach. But living in that kind of cognitive dissonance wasn't serving me. So I created some boundaries for myself.

I decided that I wouldn't allow myself to drink and stay in bed for more than a week. If I couldn't get out of bed after the week, then it was time to see a doctor. That boundary did several things for me. It forced me to set a limit on my despair and my self-destructive habits, and to acknowledge that I might need professional help. While I wallowed, I felt terrible. And I didn't want to feel terrible. Something in me knew that I had to do better, and I wanted to do better.

One of my top priorities was to take better care of myself. I could see that I was incredibly unhealthy, and my stress level was through the roof. The drinking and smoking were probably the unhealthiest things I was doing—not to mention that they weren't in line with my values of moderation and my desire to model greatness to my kids—but I wasn't eating either. I was so anxious and nauseated that I didn't feel like eating.

I was living on coffee. And more than a few people said, "You look great!" I was the unhealthiest I'd been in my life, and yet society rewarded me.

It was time for me to embrace authentic self-care.

As I explored and expanded the boundaries of my independence, it felt good to make progress on my terms and at my pace. I said yes to invitations and tried so many new things. My only two criteria were that whatever I said yes to had to be in line with my values, and that I show up and try my hardest no matter what the outcome or what a fool I might look while doing it. Trust me, from Zumba to twerking there was many a fail, but there were many more wins.

Discover Yourself in Self-Care

Authentic self-care isn't tied to vanity, and it's not even about self-soothing. I mean, it is soothing, but not in the numbing-out, avoidance way of the addict.

Authentic self-care reduces our stress levels and helps us get physically fit and healthier, but the reason I emphasize it here is that it ties into the internal work we're doing. It helps us determine what the most accessible, meaningful, and doable thing is that will create the momentum we need to keep going.

As we identify our core values and find what makes us happy, what recharges our batteries, we'll create new rituals and routines that will comfort and empower us to be the person we want to be.

Every time I participate in outside coaching conventions and retreats, there's buzz about self-care, meditation, and mindfulness. My first taste of mindfulness and the power of small wins came when I willed myself out of bed one day. Another day I was able to breathe more. And on another day I made food for myself instead of drinking coffee on an empty stomach. Mindfulness was not only healing but also a way to build a resilience deep within and a mental horsepower that kept me focused and on track. Bargaining and denial faded, and I moved into anger and sadness.

Hey, it ain't pretty, but it's reality.

That might not sound encouraging, but it is. It's movement. It got me two steps closer to my authentic self and a life I couldn't even dream of at that point but knew had to be better than what I was experiencing.

Mindfulness is an easier word to take in because it's more passive. Self-care is something that can be harder because we must act. We must take responsibility for what we're doing or not doing. It's not hard to see why it's so important. It can even be energizing to make an aspirational list: get a massage once a month, wake up at 6 a.m. every day, meditate. But there can be a lot of pressure about it. There's an emphasis on the practice itself. The routine.

Why do we have to work out three times a week?

Why do we have to restrict certain foods or calories?

Why do we need to chew X number of times and sit on a mat for X number of minutes?

When we adopt this kind of rules-based mindset, we put a lot of pressure on ourselves.

Again, we're taking someone else's ideal, their version of what is and isn't good, and putting it on. If we're trying it on for size, that's one thing. But if we're lost and trying to take a shortcut to authenticity by putting on someone else's—albeit healthier—lifestyle, we're not moving forward in a meaningful and sustainable way. We're setting up a pass or fail situation. The first day we don't make it to the gym, we fail. And then we're right back into that energy. And that sucks. That's toxic positivity in practice, doing all the right things for all the wrong reasons, and doing it with a smile on your face while you're being crushed on the inside.

Self-care is not about rules. It's about answering this question: What's the next most accessible thing I can do to take care of myself physically, mentally, and emotionally?

This allows us to reframe our decisions. You might decide on Monday afternoon that you're going to go to the gym on

Feelings can betray us, and **they can be a powerful guide.**

Tuesday but then have a conversation with your former partner that keeps you from sleeping that night. If on Tuesday you feel drained and overstimulated, the next most accessible thing for you might be to take a bath. In that case, you're choosing the self-care of rest. Or maybe you choose to go for a walk instead. Skip the gym. That's fine. Own that as your self-care moment instead of judging yourself as being lazy or not serious about your health and well-being.

In those early days, going for a walk would have felt like running a 5K. My next most accessible thing as I lay on my bed was to get up and wash my face. I'd do that, and then ask myself what my next most accessible thing was. Put up my hair. Okay, done. Now what? Put comfies on. Some days, all I could do was focus on breathing.

We don't have to outsource self-care. We don't have to pay for memberships. We often don't have to leave the house. When it comes to physical activity, I don't like to work out, but I do like to be active. I do like to feel my power and learn new things.

These were some of the things on my list, and I encourage my clients to think about them too:

- Sit outside.
- Go for a hike.
- Read a book.
- Join a book club.
- Visit an art museum.
- Work in your garden.
- Volunteer at an animal shelter.

In the beginning, everything I did was at home. Baths were important to me. It was a way to take care of myself. Taking care of houseplants was incredibly rewarding. They helped me be more comfortable in my space. The more I did, the more capable and confident I felt, which allowed me to add the next thing to my self-care menu.

The exercise aspect of self-care is not optional. What's happening in our minds plays out in our bodies. I was getting sick, and it was clear that I was suffering from emotional blockages. If I didn't cleanse my system, it would fail. When I was ready to venture beyond the threshold of what had been our family home, I took the opportunity to explore my options and figure out what I like.

Having just had a baby, I was dealing with abdominal separation and pelvic floor issues so I couldn't stress my body too much. I decided to try Pilates. I was doing it as injury therapy, but the class I chose provided unexpected benefits.

The daytime Pilates class I had selected attracted shift workers and retired people, all women. The class delivered on the physical benefits I'd expected and so much more. Even though I was the youngest by far, the class introduced me to an entirely new social network and perspective. It taught me to look at every experience available to me and make purposeful choices about how I engaged. I decided that, no matter what I tried, I would show up and try with all my effort.

I did it all—Zumba, Pilates, tennis lessons, you name it. Through that experimental phase, I realized that I preferred small group drop-in classes (the ones with no membership required). I didn't stop with fitness. I pressed further into health and wellness. I tried acupuncture, retreats, massages, facials, and a few other girl things that I'll talk more about in chapter 16.

Regardless of your body type or your abilities, budget, and time constraints, you have options related to your physical health, your mental health, your nurturing side, all the things you need. The possibilities are limited only by your willingness to find yourself by doing the next thing.

A New Way of Being with Ourselves

In those early days of awakening to my authentic self, it was more comfortable for me to be alone while I worked on myself. I did go to a doctor for support, but I also got in a self-help loop, which allowed me to make progress on my own terms. Had I gotten to know myself sooner and explored earlier, maybe it wouldn't have taken me so long to improve my life.

So what if it takes some people two years or three years or five years. This mindfulness stuff requires us to listen and lean into discomfort. It's about stepping out of the skin we were wearing, and getting comfortable in our own skin.

If you're like me, you might be identifying with your authentic self for the first time. It takes getting used to. For every time you've done something one way, someone else's way, you're going to have to practice it the new way—your way. It's incredibly hard, so remember that you're only required to do the next accessible thing.

3

. . . . .

This Thing's Too Big to Do Alone

PILED ONTO the physical and emotional stress of a new baby and post-partum depression was the pressure of the secrecy under which I had to live.

Our separation under the same roof was in full swing, but to the outside observer little had changed. The changes in our patterns of behaviour that were visible to others could be easily explained by the recent addition to our family and my recovery from it.

I couldn't turn to family because Lee and I hadn't made any long-term decisions yet. Behind the scenes we lived our broken, complicated, miserable lives. My chosen girlfriend that I trusted with my secret was shocked when I explained what was happening. Tears ran down her face.

Somehow this was both comforting and worrisome. It confirmed that I wasn't crazy or overreacting and that the situation was serious. She recognized that I needed help and that the help needed to be professional. I appreciated her objectivity. This was too big for my friends. I needed professional support so I could avoid pulling my friends down with me.

Ask for Help

I didn't know where to start, so I made an appointment with my doctor. I explained to her that I was depressed, and that my husband was struggling. You know, young family, new baby coming home kinda stuff, I said. It was as much as I could share while keeping my dirty little secret from anyone, even from myself. The truth is I just couldn't speak it out loud because I felt like that would breathe life into my worst nightmare.

My denial was profound. My doctor dug deeper, recognizing that I was never in her office unless it mattered. She tried to help me see my need. I was depressed, anxious, sleep-deprived, and trying to process the dissolution of my ten-year marriage. Looking back, I see that while she was focused on me and my mental health, I was focused on my husband and my marriage.

I could not even identify with mental health and wellness being an issue. I was not one of *those* people. I was just sad and healing from pregnancy and delivery. Stigmas associated with mental health issues are real. I felt alone. I felt guilt and shame for not being able to get my shit together and just figure it out.

She gave me the names of several local mental health professionals. I didn't contact them. I didn't trust that they would respect doctor-patient confidentiality. But that was just an excuse to not face reality. My shame about my perceived failure as a wife gripped me so tightly that I was only able to focus on trying to be better, to be good enough to save what I knew deep down was already lost.

Sometimes our pain is so overwhelming that we simply cannot see a way to move forward. We're paralyzed by the flood of feelings and don't know when and if we need help.

I wasn't asking for help, but thankfully my friend held me accountable to at least take the first step and call a therapist.

Eventually I made an appointment with a therapist who practiced outside my city. She helped save my life.

Licensed Therapists

There were times when I was so low that I thought about ending my life. I thought about hurting myself because maybe it would remind Lee that he did love me and he'd return to take care of me. I did convince Lee to come for a few therapy sessions, but he didn't believe that any of the homework the therapist suggested would solve our problems. He had put up a wall. I had no chance of getting over it. He was likely a few years ahead of me on the emotional curve. It didn't take him nearly as long as it took me to get to the *It's over* line, but he was slow to walk out the door.

His body language, tone, and communication changed. He distanced himself in every interaction. If I came in a room, he went out. He spent more and more time outside of the home. He was deeply unhappy, but I think he was giving me time and space to catch up to the reality of our marriage ending.

I thought about running away temporarily or moving away indefinitely. My therapist talked me through my thoughts and feelings and helped define the root of my unhappiness. And it had everything to do with me. I was the problem, and I was the solution.

I chose a licensed therapist who had the training and tools necessary to meet me where I was and guide me forward, and we developed a schedule that fit my needs. I specifically chose a marriage and family therapist with a coaching mindset.

I worked with her weekly for two years and then monthly for two years, and to this day have a place for her in my calendar. During that time, I slowly carved out new routines and developed new rituals. She helped me define goals and figure out how to achieve them. I learned how to avoid being activated and to recover when I was. I didn't go it alone.

I wanted to work with someone who had a lot of information and resources and could break down my psychology, the ins and outs of my behaviours. She gave me all that, but I also wanted the two of us to define a list of goals and set a pace to accomplish them. I wanted her support as I marched toward those goals. One thing I did not want was to get stuck in what I see as minutiae. Often women will come to me and say, "My goodness, I was just so tired of sitting in a therapist's office crying about the past while seeing no discernible path forward." These women, like me, are not interested in the traditional therapy model that feels like a slow psychological peeling back of the layers, going back into one's childhood and exploring every nook and cranny of the psyche.

But that's exactly what some people need to do, so I encourage you to be curious and to not expect an immediate fit or think that your co-worker swearing by her therapist means the same choice will be right for you. You may not even need a therapist. You may need another type of supportive professional.

Life and Soul Coaches

In addition to seeing a licensed family therapist, I found it helpful to hire a soul coach. Soul coaches help their clients tap into their intuition, which helps them discover their authentic self.

Coaching can help get you unstuck, and many people hire life and business coaches at times of crisis or when they

Sometimes our pain is so overwhelming that we simply **cannot see a way to move forward.**

want to make significant positive changes. Some therapists operate with a coaching mindset, but coaches are not therapists or counsellors unless they have the proper education and licenses.

I make it clear when people come to me for guidance that there are things I can do and things I can't. Recently a client told me that she was being abused. I immediately told her that it was good she was asking for help because she shouldn't go it alone under those circumstances, but I also made sure she was receiving support from the right people and organizations.

Arguably, the primary distinction between licensed therapists and coaches is that coaches tend to focus on where clients are at any given time and what it will take to get them from where they are to where they want to be. When I work with clients, I'm candid. I say, "Here are the straight goods." I offer my opinion based on personal experience and the collection of shared experiences I've logged with clients who are in similar situations.

Like therapists, coaches don't have the biases that our friends, family, and associates have. You'll likely find more Type As working with a coach than more laid-back types because many coaches—myself included—are process driven. Many of the women I work with are community leaders, CEOs, and highly organized stay-at-home moms. Give us data and give us tools, and we'll go to work. We may ugly cry all the way through the task, but by God, we are in control!

But as any Type A (and the people who love them) will tell you, Type As will often channel their frustration and negative energy into a new challenge. This can be counterproductive. They're often the ones who either punish or neglect their mental and physical health as they focus on a different goal.

Health and Wellness Support

If you've neglected your physical health, of course, focus on that as much as you focus on your mental health. Take this opportunity to get that Pap smear, have those boobs squished at the mammogram station, have a dentist polish those pearly whites. Trust me. You'll feel great. And these are normal things to do that shouldn't take you too far out of your comfort zone.

If you're up for it, have a massage or a facial. And if you burst into tears, that's okay. It's probably not the first time that's happened to your wellness pro.

Remember that none of this is about improving your appearance or prepping you to jump back into the dating pool to meet someone new. This is one hundred percent about healing and getting comfortable in your own skin. If you so choose, the time will come for fitness regimens and coochy tightening (yep, done it), but we'll save that fun stuff for later because the first steps you take away from the person you thought was your forever person are hard, and now's the time to focus on an inside out approach.

Accept Your Vulnerability

This moment of tragedy in your life is—I promise—an incredible opportunity to grow through grief. Even if you think you're coping well on your own, I encourage anyone who can to find professional support through something like this because you're in crisis. You are vulnerable. Each person's crisis is different, along with the vulnerabilities it exposes. Each of us has our own values, personalities, constraints, and opportunities. Finding the right fit for our area(s) of need is critical, and I found that the process helped me to overcome even more fear and to take responsibility for what my authentic self was asking of me.

There is, of course, a lot you can and must do on your own. But when it comes to your body and your mind, it's important that you're supported on your journey to physical and emotional health and self-discovery.

4

· · · · ·

Unwife

WITH THE stroke of a pen our marriage was over, and my failure as a wife was on the record. At least I was getting out of bed every day and had ditched the smoking and drinking. But I still struggled with my identity outside of being Lee's wife.

It's not like I had a lot of warm and fuzzy feelings for him, and many of my clients can relate. This stage in the break-up is hard, hard, hard, because there's been a major shift away from couplehood but there can still be a lot of interaction. To be constantly faced with that is taxing, exhausting even. We can be activated in a nanosecond.

If we're self-aware and doing the work to connect with our core values and model greatness, we start to take the emotion out of things and we don't take our ex's actions as personally. This is about adopting the mindset of unwifing.

To be clear, I am not pro divorce. But if divorce is our reality, we've got to uncouple physically, mentally, and emotionally.

Break the Cycle of Blame

As I processed the shock, pain, and fear during our separation and immediately after our divorce, I felt like I was getting knocked down every time I tried to stand up. My children were frustrated and upset; I was wading through professional divorce jargon and processes and interactions I really didn't want to have. I often felt like a punching bag.

When something activated me, I'd get rage-y and emotional but usually not in a productive, gotta-move-my-self-through-this way. I'd flip back into wife and unhealthy mom mode. Specifically, if Lee wasn't feeling well or if he was really stressed about work or any other thing and wasn't able to show up for the kids, I'd start running interference. To watch the man I loved suffer and my kids suffer placed me in the problem-solver, peacemaker mode when I needed that energy and time to take care of the stuff in my heart and on my plate.

I finally realized that it's not my job to help him or solve any of the problems associated with him. If we take those things on, the other person will never stand up and take responsibility. Why should they?

When we disproportionately allocate thoughts and emotional bandwidth to someone who's now part of our past, we can't look forward. We will always be in victim mode. I had to tell myself often and I now tell my clients often: *Let their shit go.* And stop talking about it to yourself and the people around you because when you're talking about the other person, you're actually putting that person before yourself. You're choosing to continue to make the other person a priority.

One measure of how over someone or something you are is how much you talk about them or it. As soon in this process as you can, take responsibility for yourself and purposefully avoid bearing other people's burdens. It's too much and ultimately doesn't do you or your children any good.

Peel Off Those Labels

There are so many reasons why people try to keep a marriage together. Nobody enjoys failure. *Wife* has a nice ring to it (no pun intended). We don't want our children to be from a broken home. With divorce comes shame and stigma. I would have rather stayed in my unhealthy marriage than face the stigma associated with being an ex-wife.

Daughter, friend, wife, mom are just job descriptions. They're not *identities*. That wife description though. It's a huge one in our society. We put such stock in being in a couple, especially what it means to be a married couple.

But when we uncouple from a marriage, we rarely take on the label of single. No, we're now an ex-wife, we're divorced. No neutral labels for us. We're broken. We're burdened with negative phrasing.

Think about how we move through our professional lives. When we change jobs, we say things like, "In my previous career..." or "In my past life as a..." We don't position things as our ex-careers or ex-jobs. Even people who've had terrible workplace experiences or were fired rarely use loaded language that hints at any failure on their part.

In keeping with that idea, I encourage women to change their vernacular. Using phrases such as *former partner* rather than *ex* not only helps break the cycle of blame, it also honours the relationship and the beautiful parts that can serve as a legacy for our children.

This may be a difficult shift in mindset and practice, especially if you have few fond memories or haven't yet identified

*What's essential?
What are you
going to carry?
More importantly,*
**what are you going
to leave behind?**

your core values and decided how you want to move through the world. Remember that this is a two-steps-forward, one-step-back journey, so if you're not with me here, don't worry. My goal is to help you find your authentic self.

To be our Self, which is to have our own identity, we must detach ourselves from all the labels and expectations other people have placed on us. Unwifing means we've got to strip down to our naked Alicia, Kirsten, Sasha, Mary, or your name here.

We must be naked and unafraid, unashamed.

If the idea of being naked is too scary a thought, here's a different way of thinking about it. A favourite meditation of mine early on was to sit and think about unpacking everything that was in the backpack I was carrying. In my mind, I'd take the pack off, lay it down, take each thing out and lay it out where I could see it. Go ahead. Do this exercise right now with me.

Now think about the massive mountain you're about to climb. There are things you need and things that take up space and add weight. What's essential? What are you going to carry? More importantly, what are you going to leave behind? The first time I did that, I thought, *Wow. I'm not putting much of that stuff back in.* So much junk. Some of it I'd picked up myself and put in my backpack, but it was also as if I'd let other people put things in my bag according to what they thought I needed based on some trip they wanted me to make.

The truth is that we get to decide what path we want to take, what mountains we'll summit, and only we can decide what monikers fit and what we'll take with us. As we peel off labels and unpack our shame, we find ourselves living in our truth and showing up one hundred percent for ourselves and for the people who truly matter.

Co-dependence, blame, and sticky labels make it easy to stay in wife mode, holding onto that title and those patterns of thought because, let's face it, when we were in that partnership, we would talk about our former partner all the time. Of course we did, because that person was the most significant person in our lives. But if you're still talking about that person frequently or with strong feelings, you're stuck. I remember my therapist asking how often we text. When I replied "daily," she shared that this was too much and it didn't create space for healing and recovery. I shared this with Lee and we started to text weekly instead—what a difference to my personal ability to move forward without attachments.

Embrace Autonomy

Many of us have been guilted and shamed into staying married. Even if it's not outright, the social and familial pressure is certainly felt. That pressure can perpetuate resentment and anger, which makes for nasty divorce. Instead of it being an acceptable thing like changing jobs or selling our house and moving to another, we feel pressured from all sides to stay. In almost every way, coupled adults lose their ability to relate to single adults in normal and human ways. So, it's to be expected that we're going to struggle—even for those of us in relatively good emotional states—with the idea of being our single selves.

The good news is that you already know you have to face your fears, and hopefully you've embraced self-care and are supported by professionals. You're defining your values and finding your authentic self, and you have been adding good things to your life that are taking the time and place of your former partner. You're focusing on thoughts and actions that make you feel the way you want to feel, and now it's time to embrace all of that and put measurable space between what was *we* and what is now *you*.

It's time to develop an extreme focus on you and the things you can control. If you don't, your life will continue to be about you and that other person, you alongside someone else. Seeing yourself as an autonomous human is empowering! You choose your values and how to act them out in any given situation. You choose if you want spaghetti or SpaghettiOs, if you want to watch *French Kiss* or *The French Connection*. You. You. Glorious you!

You're going to have setbacks for sure, but as you move past conforming to another person's idea (or your idea of that person's idea) of right or utilitarian behaviour, you'll stop second-guessing yourself. You'll start to recognize your abilities and see yourself as the capable woman you are. Building your confidence and sense of self-worth is an ongoing thing. Trust that you know a lot of stuff and can do for yourself because, whether you believe it or not, you now *have* to do for yourself.

In any conversation about unwifing, it's important to step back and remember that being alone is not the same thing as being lonely. We can be alone but not lonely, just like we can be surrounded by people and feel alone.

In the months after Lee and I divorced, I often felt that alone and lonely were one and the same. Being on my own with the kids was incredibly isolating. I tried so hard to be strong in front of them, but I felt like I was being crushed. I often found myself fighting to hold my tears inside, feeling like my throat would explode. When the kids left to spend time with their dad, I would wave and blow a million kisses. From the outside, I looked happy and like I was kicking this divorce's butt. Until the door shut. Then I'd curl up in a ball, sobbing for what felt like hours.

What was my life without my family? I had no idea how unhealthy my dependence on people had become. My entire identity was wrapped up in other people. Embracing sounds so easy. Just a hug, right? So warm, so comforting. Wow. *So* not that at times. But I hope you feel my compassion as you read this book, because all along the way my divorce taught me extreme lessons. The great thing was, and is—and I'll keep saying it because it's so important to remember—that finding myself and seeing myself as a whole person, apart from and sometimes in spite of any other person, led me to experience life in ways I couldn't have imagined at the time.

The Next Stage

Now it's time for you to start engaging with the outside world in meaningful ways and putting into practice the lessons you've learned in semi-isolation. Life will force you to, and the rest of this book will encourage and prepare you to get out of your cocoon, spread your wings, and fly.

It's not going to be comfortable, but it's time. It's time to get on with life and figure out what parts of your old life still fit and which parts and people need to go. And the beautiful thing is that if you've started doing all the things we've talked about so far, you'll have the momentum you need to roll on to the next thing.

two
. . . .

NO NEED TO CHANGE, JUST EVOLVE

5

· · · · ·

Be the
Leading Lady

EVERY WINTER for five years, Lee's business sponsored
the biggest fundraiser in our community. People showed
up in large numbers and with big hearts. I *loved* that
fundraiser. It gave me all the feels. I especially loved
that Lee and I did it as a couple. But when it happened in
2016, I wasn't a part of that couple anymore.

Not being able to show up to that event on my husband's
arm was devastating on several levels. I was heartbroken
about not experiencing the event alongside him, and I was
left to wonder what part I should play.

I could choose to not go, to avoid the self-doubt and discomfort by putting that thing I loved in my past along with
my marriage. I could be a victim, a martyr. I could be jealous
and frail. Or I could cajole myself into going just to show up
and say I'd done it.

The first year after my divorce, I just couldn't face it. I
didn't want to be judged and feel like I was on display. So,
I participated but didn't go to the party. I worked behind

the scenes as a volunteer. I was visible backstage during the lead-up but absent on the night of the event. The spotlight (real or imagined) was too much for me.

But the following year, I chose a different way to show up. I was there centre stage.

My a-ha moment came while watching the 2006 film *The Holiday*, starring Cameron Diaz and Kate Winslet and written by Nancy Meyers. It's the story of two women who are both trying to get over—I'll give you one guess—a man in their lives. Each has suffered a heartbreak, and each thinks that switching houses and scenery (one lives in L.A., the other in England) during the holidays will jolt them out of their misery and reboot their lives. Of course, it doesn't work that way.

In one scene, after Kate Winslet's character has an emotional breakdown about her ex-boyfriend, the movie producer she's dining with tells her that there are two kinds of character tropes in the movies: leading ladies and best friends. "You, I can tell, are a leading lady," he says. "But for some reason, you're behaving like the best friend." Sitting there in my jammies by myself that first Christmas, I thought, *That's it. Why have I not shown up as the leading lady in my own life, in my own story and my own movie?*

You might think that was a bitter pill to swallow, but it wasn't. It was freeing. I was ready to take myself seriously and take the next step in my hero's journey. Just because we're assigned a role (or because we took one out of fear) doesn't mean we can't rewrite the damn script. Sure, life is always going to surprise us. But our journey doesn't stop until we say it stops.

Leading ladies engage in dialogue. They don't play small. They don't react from a place of fear. They don't succumb to limiting beliefs. Leading ladies show up and, one way or another, entertain and inspire those around them. They step into the spotlight.

Leading ladies know that the show must go on, and that they are the star.

Think like a Director

Two years after my divorce, I was still a patron of the fund-raiser. And I could see what I needed to do.

Every year, all of the tables at the event were couples' tables. This would no longer do. I thought, *I'm going to own this, and if I'm coming back on the scene, there'll be no mistaking what I want or who I am.* I was not going to minimize my leading lady part by sitting down at a couples' table, looking all awkward and alone. Instead, I sponsored a ladies-only table. It had never been done, so that's what I did.

What do leading ladies and power players do when they don't like the role they've been assigned or the words someone else wants to put in their mouths? They rewrite the script.

Was I nervous when I arrived, knowing that I would be in a familiar setting but no longer familiar to me? Absolutely.

Did I know that some people in the audience would be watching me, judging me, and revelling in the prospect of drama? Hell yes.

Did I see my place on the stage and know exactly what to do when I got there? *Hell yeah!*

I was one hundred percent in my authentic self—at an event I wanted to be part of, doing what I wanted, and in a way that fit my personality and new situation.

How do you get comfortable with discomfort and learn to navigate an ever-changing world and develop confidence as we do it? You think like a director and block your scenes. You move across the stage and engage with other actors in predictable ways whenever you can.

In this case, the event room was the set. The table was where I staked my claim, owned my space. But I knew I wouldn't be able to stay at that table all night. I'd be mixing and mingling because that's what people do at these things and that's what I do at these things. That's me being authentic me. But even us mixers and minglers still love a table, and it's easier to mix and mingle when you're in a couple. It gives you a person to go to or stand with as you enter and leave a group, and it also gives you an automatic out of awkward or tedious conversations: "Oh, looks like the husband needs some help, better go do my duty," or simply that *Save me!* signal that triggers your wingman to come and tactfully rescue you.

Standing alone in a crowded room is one of the most intimidating situations a person can find themselves in. When I'm left all by my lonesome with only a cocktail to keep me company, I want to run, recoil. But with practice, I did learn how to engage in conversation with people, and to feel more capable and confident as I navigated this familiar stage in my new role.

At first, as I found my footing in social situations, I'd go to the bathroom when an awkward alone moment arrived. Do something. Go get another drink, participate in any kind of group activity that was happening. A social anxiety mantra I adopted was *When in doubt, look busy.* But there's one thing about writing and acting and the creative life that we must never lose sight of: At the end of the day, life and art are a collaborative affair.

Our performance will always be influenced to one degree or another by the other actors on set. I realized that people would be curious about the break-up of a couple that had seemed so perfect. They'd ask questions I didn't want to or wasn't ready to answer. I also realized that looking busy and talking about the food would only get me so far. So when I decided to attend that fundraiser, I understood that the experience would require me to do some improvisation.

*At the end
of the day,
life and art are*
**a collaborative
affair.**

Learn to Improvise

We're talking about saying *yes* to life. *Yes* can be scary. *Yes* can be awkward. Correction. It *is* scary, and it *is* awkward. When going through a divorce, the first question that pops into our minds when faced with this new stage is often: *How do I go out into this world alone?*

You just do.

Not everything in life is scripted. Life is all the things, right? All the opportunities to experience people and situations. Some of those things still have to do with our pre-existing life, the one that's still there but the relationships have changed. We're still doing things with but not *with* our former partner because we share friends and maybe a business or kids or a dog, or you live in a one-horse prairie-dog town and can't help but run into each other at the Grocery Garage or the Pedicure Palace. No matter what our situation, there's a whole new life that we have to show up to all by ourselves. I've found that when you don't know what to do or say, the best thing is to simply say yes, and try everything. It's the improv mindset of *yes and*.

Instead of reacting with a fearful hard *no*, which shuts the thinking brain down, actors are taught to embrace a *yes and* mindset when faced with a question or challenge. They immediately say *yes* to the situation, then ask themselves what they can add to it—the *and* part. This way, they allow themselves to get comfortable with discomfort. It's what I call mindful change management.

The only constant is change, right? So, we might as well get used to it.

As I embraced the idea that change can be good and let go of my need to control every situation, I started to recognize and rely on my intuition. Now, I observe my intuition.

I look at it until I'm ready to listen to it. As I got better and better at doing this, I realized that distancing my thoughts and actions from my Self had resulted in me being light years from my intuition. I had built up so many layers and walls to compartmentalize any type of feeling. Once, after explaining to my soul coach why something wasn't working and could never work (i.e., my lizard brain saying, "Um, no. Hard pass, but thanks"), my coach looked at me and said, "Wow, you sure do over-intellectualize everything." That was a nice way of saying, among other things, that my ego was out of control.

Over-thinking kills creativity. And it'll kill confidence dead, dead, dead.

There's no place for ego on stage. The heat of the anger, jealousy, and cowardice that lives in ego burns the other actors and make the audience uncomfortable. Ego is insecurity disguised as confidence.

The night of the fundraiser inevitably arrived. Standing in that room, surrounded by a steady, hundreds-deep flow of friends, colleagues, acquaintances, and strangers, all looking to engage and make an impact on this night and for our community, filled me with excitement and anticipation. I was scared as fuck. But it wasn't the kind of fear that had held back my desire to dream, to be bold, and to embrace adventure. It wasn't the fear that had caused anxiety and post-partum depression, or that had fuelled my desire for safe and comfortable at any cost. This was different, like the molten core of my authentic self. This was an energy that helped me channel my intuition. It might have warned me to take a healthy pause before moving forward, but it wanted me to move forward nonetheless.

As I moved through the room that night, I thought about that piece of self-help advice we often hear: "Fake it till you make it."

The pen we used to sign those divorce papers **is the same one we can use to ink the next act in our life's story.**

But I wasn't faking it. I was practicing being my Self. It only felt fake at first because I had been acting a part written for someone else. And I had been doing it for so long that I had not yet become comfortable with playing the part I wanted to play.

Fake It till You Make It Is Bullshit

"Fake it till you make it" is dangerous advice because often the people who apply it are measuring themselves according to someone else's definition of success. It puts us right back in our old situation, and it is powered by ego, not authenticity.

Beware of toxic positivity. Yes, sometimes we must smile and act the part, but this isn't about *acting* like a leading lady. It's about *being* the leading lady. If you can't own it, if a role doesn't match your authentic self, don't take it.

To be a leading lady, we must lead. This is all emotional. It's one thing to manage change. It's another to use it to shape ourselves and our lives into something we want. As humans, we'll never shake our emotions. We'll always feel vulnerable when we experience new situations and meet new people. But if we can see ourselves as actors, not fakers, we can step out of ourselves and help ourselves through any set of circumstances.

When I realized that "fake it till you make it" is bullshit advice, I became acutely aware of it. When I drifted back toward people who are all about status and money and power and superficial things, I could smell it. It reminded me that I didn't want to fake it till I made it according to their definitions of success. I want to show up as my authentic self and interact with other humans who are showing up as their authentic selves. Now I surround myself with people who seek meaningful connection through shared experiences, people who want to make a difference in the world and be happy.

The reality is that many of the things that happen in our lives, good or bad, are unexpected. We welcome the fun, exciting surprises in life, but, against all rational thought, we're shocked and dismayed when something bad happens.

The narratives we attach to divorce are almost always negative. In fact, divorce is a catalyst for change. I say, let life surprise you. Life is supposed to be exciting, right? We humans are always saying we want new and novel experiences, right? Spontaneity is the spice of life, after all! Then let's let life surprise us. This life is an exciting one, and the pen we used to sign those divorce papers is the same one we can use to ink the next act in our life's story. And we're just entering act two. It's not like we have to have all our shit together right now. (That would make for a boring story anyway.) We just need to see ourselves as leading ladies and start to see the possibilities of what's to come without trying to control it.

Cast Yourself in the Role

There's a time for everything: a time for improvisation and a time for preparation and mindful stage blocking. Learning to trust your gut by practicing both—while still within the relative safety of your normal life and peer group—is a confidence booster like no other and will prepare you for bigger stages.

But without self-awareness and situational awareness, it's very easy to slip back into a supporting role—especially for mothers, because it's socially acceptable and even encouraged for us to put our children first in everything we do. It's important to remember that casting ourselves as the leading lady isn't about putting our needs over the needs of people who are dependent upon us. It's about taking the stage with pride and dignity and being the hero of our own journey.

The clearer we are about who we want to be and the physical, spiritual, and emotional journey we want our character to go through, the more we'll show up in life as the leading lady. We won't live through and for other people anymore. Supporting actors in friend roles do that. This is our story, our movie.

6

. . . . .

Find Your Voice

EVEN WHEN we identify who we are and what we want, we need to have a clear line of sight and know what our priorities are at any given time and when interacting with any given person. We must practice healthy boundaries and communicate what we need or want. The consequences for not doing so are dire.

Many people—especially women—were never taught how to defend their beliefs or assert themselves in conversations. We're the peacekeepers, the nurturers, the cheerleaders, the passive ones. We advocate for others but don't know what to expect when we find ourselves in need of advocacy.

When facing separation or divorce, we don't always know how other people are going to react, what they're going to ask or, perhaps worse, what they might project onto us. This makes it challenging to speak up, not to mention that some of us take awhile to process information or feel like we always need to have and give an answer (and the-whole-truth-and-nothing-but-the-truth one at that).

Many of the women I coach say things like, "I know who I am. I know my values. But this is the first time I've really thought about what healthy boundaries are." What they don't yet see or understand is how to establish their boundaries in the minds of others. A fence with a locked gate is a tangible boundary, but *boundaries* in this context are almost never visible—there are no "Private Property Do Not Enter" signs, no fence, no moat. The follow-up question is often "How do I have the confidence to speak up for myself?"

What my clients are really asking is how to develop the communication skills that will support living in alignment with who they are and what they want, and how to help others understand—or at least accept—those things too. They need those skills, because they're the leading lady and the boss of their life, and they're on a journey to living an authentic life and to being a model of greatness.

Redirect the Conversation

When it comes to communication, the antithesis of greatness is gossip. And let's face the facts. We humans are curious. We love gossip. Regardless of gender, we want the 411.

One of the things we do to feed that need is to ask broad questions. If you haven't already, I'd bet money that you'll soon hear questions like this one I once got: "Well, what happened?"

I mean, come on. Do I really want to sit down and go over three years or fifteen years of partnership? No. No, I do not. And why the hell do people ask these prying, open-ended questions at kids' birthday parties, PTA meetings, or in aisle 5 of Walmart?

First, the people who ask are almost always married. When confronted by questions like this, I used to say, "Really? You're married. I don't think I have to tell you what happened. You know."

Second, nosiness is often disguised as concern and compassion: the offer of a shoulder to cry on in exchange for some dirt. Don't fall for it.

Another crowd favourite is "How's [insert name of your former partner] doing?"

When I sat down and documented my values (an ongoing project, by the way), I determined that one of mine is to not talk about another person's experience, because that's their story to tell. I wouldn't want just anyone—and certainly not my former or soon-to-be-former partner—to interpret my situation and assume my thoughts and feelings and share those with others as fact. Even though I did know details and even though there were things I could have said, it was my choice to shut that type of inquiry down.

So, I realized I needed to have some kind of statement that I could say in these situations. I landed on this casual response that has served me well: "Oh, hey, I saw him the other day. I think he's doing great, but you'd have to ask him that."

Asked and answered. Next question, please.

This works well when people talk *at* us too (almost like they're trying to show us they care and understand by putting words in our mouths), or when they start to label things. When someone says "ex," I have the opportunity to jump in and say, "Oh, actually, I prefer to think of Lee as my former partner, co-parent, or my kids' dad." If someone uses the phrase "broken home" or any other negative or divisive language or focuses on the negative impacts of divorce on women and children, I reframe that conversation.

I like to think of these as elevator pitches, those answers that are short enough to give on an elevator ride between floors. They're really handy. In the beginning I kept a mental stack queued up anytime I knew I might run into people with big ears and loose lips.

There were some nights when I could speak about it and other nights when I couldn't. I assembled my elevator pitches accordingly. Even on the nights I could talk about it in a positive way, doing so quickly depleted my energy. Having those pre-determined elevator pitches ready to go has helped me relax and enjoy my time with people. They can reduce those awkward moments when we find ourselves alone in a crowded social setting too. When I'm at an event, I can always go find a mom and, as boring as it is sometimes, ask them about their kids.

Redirecting and finding common ground can help us find our voices.

Today, I have the confidence to share my perspectives and interests with the world because I feel good being me and no longer worry about the judgement of others. I know my values now, and how I want to use my words. I have a set of topics I can throw out as conversation starters, and I am comfortable starting or redirecting any conversation.

Use Present and Future Tense, Not Past

It's one thing to go to a party or out to the shops in a mindful state and with prepackaged answers to predictable questions. It's quite another to know what to say when your guard is down and you're talking to long-time couple friends.

For a period of time even after I was fairly well practiced in conversational boundaries and redirecting, I'd often catch myself talking about my former husband. It wasn't negative talk. It would be anecdotal stuff. It was what I felt our friends cared about in terms of a point of reference. After all, we'd experienced so much of our lives together.

Once, I got into a conversation with old friends about travel, and a flood of memories came rushing to mind. Of

Nothing worth talking about ever happens while **sitting alone at a table in the corner.**

course, Lee was in all of them. Many of the stories were about things we did and how much we loved this or that. It felt natural to talk about those things, but I wondered how I'd talk about my life to people who didn't know that Lee no longer existed in my world as my husband.

My friend's husband, whom I'd always loved and respected, looked at me and said, "Well... how do I say this? I think you got on the bus and Lee didn't, and you've got to keep taking the bus as it drives forward. There are stops ahead for you, but Lee's not on the bus anymore." As soon as he said it, my stomach clenched, and my face got hot. I was so embarrassed because my mind translated it to "I'm not interested in your past with that person, Alicia. You need to move forward."

Guys are often more direct than us gals, a good thing in many ways. After I took a moment to process what he said, to listen to his intent and apply it to my life with self-awareness, gratitude replaced my embarrassment. I think my friend was offering a reminder that Lee and I were not travelling in the same direction anymore.

I still felt the discomfort of not being one hundred percent clear about who I was and what I wanted. My interests were still hard to pin down, and I wasn't sure exactly where I wanted to go in life. I saw myself standing at the back window of the bus, staring behind when I should have been eagerly facing forward to the rolling banner that tells us where we're going.

Message received. Great. Got it. I needed to turn in the right direction and start living a life worth talking about. To live in the moment, while looking to the future.

I definitely want to travel (not my friend's point, but one thought led to another), and so I wondered, *How do I travel if I don't have a partner to travel with?* Our culture is so ingrained with this idea of couplehood and the celebration of couplehood that it's hard to be single in any practical sense.

It's hard to talk about experiences without talking about who we shared them with.

I wasn't ready for the future, but I could handle thinking in the present tense. I needed to find some people. Any people (as long as they weren't named Lee). As luck would have it, I soon had the opportunity to travel to Montreal for a business group meeting. I travelled alone and went in a day early. I wanted to do my own thing and take in the local scene and culture. I ended up at a restaurant and, for the first time ever, I sat at the bar.

I've eaten alone many times for various reasons, but I'd always ask for a corner table and, shortly after sitting down, I'd get out my phone or start reading a book. I reached for whatever was handy to avoid looking lonely or out of place. When the host would ask, "Do you want to eat at the bar or at a table?" I would nearly panic. I didn't know how to participate at the bar.

But in Montreal, I decided that nothing worth talking about ever happens while sitting alone at a table in the corner, and I figured what the heck. Sitting at the bar offered a world of new experiences where I could be on my own but part of the world around me. What's especially fun about sitting at the bar is the opportunity to banter. The talk is about the weather, the game on the TV, the drink orders. It's in-the-moment stuff and a great way to practice self-awareness and conversational skills in a low-risk environment.

Say What You Need

While I was working on this chapter, my editor told me about a solo dining experience she once had. Although she was in a relationship at the time, she wanted to take herself on a date to her favourite Korean restaurant.

It's hard to talk about experiences without talking **about who we shared them with.**

When she sat down, the owner asked the inevitable questions: "Just one?" With a big smile on her face, she said, "Yes. I'm on a date with myself." She ordered all her favourite things and settled in for a relaxed, quiet dinner at which she could allow her mind to wander.

Things didn't go to plan. As the owner delivered each course, he lingered. It was nice at first. When he brought her tea, they chatted about their tertiary connection through a family member and how well the restaurant was doing. She didn't think much of the exchange until he brought the next course and gave a detailed explanation about the differences between cabbage and potato kimchi.

He hardly left her alone for the two hours she was there. His unspoken message was loud and clear. He felt sorry for her because she was eating alone and seemed to feel some kind of responsibility to entertain her even though her posture and openness expressed confidence, not neediness.

She walked in relaxed and hopeful and walked out irritated, frustrated, and hungry. I mean, who can eat with someone leaning over them?

Attitude and body language communicate a lot, but only to people who are paying attention. Let's face it: Most people are focused more on their own appearance and feelings than on those of others. When subtlety doesn't work, we must clearly articulate our needs.

You can always say, "Hey, if I tip you really well, will you shut up and leave me alone?" But that's unkind. No matter what, be kind! Choosing kindness is about more than the act. It's about living intentionally. It's easy to get lost in being a victim, in martyrdom, or in a woe-is-me complex. It's easy to lash out with anger or condescension. But this journey isn't about conquering situations and people. It's about walking and talking with strength, dignity, and compassion—

for ourselves and for others. It's about learning that it's okay to have needs and wants and to express them in a timely and appropriate manner.

Yes, be mindful of what your face and body are communicating. But even if your body language does communicate sadness or vulnerability, it's not anyone else's job to rescue you. In fact, if you've been projecting these qualities in an attempt to attract a knight in shining armour, go back to chapter 1. That's manipulation and not an expression of your authentic self. If it were, you'd have bailed on this book long before now. Pull on your big girl pants, and let's do this thing right.

The point is that sometimes you're going to go out in public in a frail state, and that's okay. It doesn't mean you need or want help. In fact, those are often the times when you may least want attention. Either way, kindly establish your desire to the person who's bumping up against the buffer you want to create for yourself.

I still have this kind of thing happen to me. One of the statements that works for me goes something like this: "I'm really enjoying time on my own right now. This conversation is great, but it's taking away from what I'd hoped to accomplish today." That sounds lofty, and I'm not going to pretend that I'm always self-possessed enough to say it that clearly, but I try to express my needs in a way that preserves my energy and doesn't threaten or hurt anyone.

It's hard to overemphasize the need to protect your time and energy at this stage, but think of it as akin to the healing process that happens when you're recovering from an illness or an injury. When we're fighting an infection or rebuilding our immune systems, we often get tired more easily because our body is reallocating energy it would normally use for more fun stuff. If you were married but don't have kiddos, that's where the similarities end, but if you have kids, your energy reserves are even more precious because you need all the voltage you can get your hands on to get yourself through this while also helping your children thrive through the change.

My energy is a gift I give myself, and it's a true gift because it allows me to better focus on my children in order to legitimately value their needs during this time. The world can drain the life out of us on a good day, and much more so on a bad one.

Finding your voice and using it to establish your limits and teach people how to treat you is a gift that keeps giving. You might get through the unwife phase and you might get through all the divorce stuff without the confidence and clarity that finding your voice brings, but you're certainly not going to be able to do the things we're going to talk about in the coming chapters without the skills to stand up and speak for yourself.

People treat you the way you let them, so take good care of yourself. Be self-aware and tune into your feelings. Know where you stand and what you need. If someone trespasses on your boundaries, kindly tell them so, not by pointing out what they did "wrong" but by expressing what you hope to get from an experience. Be direct and name your limits. Self-care is a priority, and this is part of it.

Silence Is Golden

Sometimes people think that not saying anything makes them seem weak, but the opposite is true. Think about the description "the strong, silent type." That can be us. We make clear choices by documenting our values, by constantly carrying them with us, and by examining them as we move through life. When I encounter people who seem more interested in gossip or negative talk about divorce than in productive or nurturing talk, I opt out.

First, I try to redirect. If they won't go along with that, I excuse myself: "Excuse me, I'm going to run to the bathroom," or "Excuse me a second, I'm going to go grab another drink." Of course, I never get back to them because I'm a leading lady, and I don't just grab onto the first warm body willing to share a word with me. I'm mindful of myself and have scoped out the set. I've blocked my scene. I know my lines. This is my show. And as the director, I choose not to add that person to my cast.

If someone is talking about positive things and has a solution-oriented mindset and words of wisdom to share with me, that's another story. I found that—even if they require more emotional investment because it's not me getting something off my chest but me becoming more self-aware— these kinds of conversations fill me up. They give me ideas and practical ways of dealing with specific situations I'm struggling with. They inspire and empower me, and I can do that all day long. I'm still relatively silent during such conversations, though, because I'm listening. I'm learning.

There's another reason to embrace silence, and it has more to do with strategy and self-preservation than with personal growth or leadership. If you're in the divorce discussion or negotiation phase, be extremely careful about what you share and with whom, and what emotions you attach to your words. As hard as it was (and believe me, it was *really* hard some days), I tried to never say anything that could be misconstrued. Saying too much or saying things in the wrong way to the wrong people is a great way to give away your control. Don't say or do anything that you wouldn't want brought up in a custody or financial negotiation. Always control the narrative. Play the long game.

Don't say or do anything that you wouldn't want brought up in a custody or financial negotiation. **Always control the narrative.**

I'm not saying to lie by omission or to deceive or anything even remotely like that. I'm saying think with your head, not with your wounded heart. Be strategic by controlling your emotions and taming your tongue whenever you're in the presence of another human. Stick to the facts. Stay in bounds. Yes, we all need to vent. I'll admit that I need to do a certain amount of totally rageful, nasty purging every once in a while. We're human, and while sure, bubble baths and meditation retreats are great, our species isn't as kumbaya as we'd like to believe. We need the catharsis a good rant has to offer. The question is, who are we ranting to and how frequently? Think carefully, because a social environment is not the time or place for that. Other people could overhear you. *Your kids could overhear you.*

Your children probably love their other parent, and navigating their new landscape is hard for them too. Depending on their age and maturity, hearing something like "I wish I'd never married that jackass" might make them consider the fact that had their parents not married, they never would have existed in this family. You might inadvertently be sending a message that you wish everything related to your former spouse would be wiped away. There's wisdom in the saying "If you can't say anything nice, don't say anything at all."

Text messaging and social media posting count as talking too. Arguably, these forms of communication are even riskier than talking in person. Whatever you say will be on permanent record and can and will be used against you. If you want my advice, here it is: Don't do it. Just don't. Especially if you're lubed up. I mean, for God's sake, put down the phone and step away from the Scotch.

We absolutely need to find our voice and develop the confidence to use it, but sometimes walking our talk requires more walking than talking.

Growth Requires Patience

Have I mentioned that all of this takes practice? Any growth-oriented person will tell you that you'll always be working on a couple of things at a time, because we're talking about mindset and behaviour. It's one thing to think about something. It's another thing to think about something and practice it in the comfort and safety of our own homes or with mature, safe people who know and love us. It's a whole 'nother animal to do all this stuff in new or changing environments and around people who are indifferent or openly hostile to our goals.

I feel like I've been working on this my whole life. Reprogramming our minds and willing ourselves into new patterns of behaviour, new habits, are so dang hard. But once we master something—no, once we are within sight of mastery—our fears melt away. The discomfort fades. We feel the power of our new independent mindset and we understand that we are tough enough and smart enough and worthy enough to do the work.

Never underestimate the power of small wins. Practice how you speak to yourself, to your friends, to your former partner. Yes, you're going to feel like a toddler learning to walk. Yes, you're going to feel vulnerable, but that's normal. This is about stepping into your own so you can face what's ahead mindfully, confidently, and with the right people.

Remember that you're likely in a weird space right now, a space between your old group of friends and associates and the group you'll eventually settle into. Improving your communication skills will help you get through this time gracefully and with as little drama as possible.

7

· · · · ·

Find Your
Inner Circle

N HER book *Braving the Wilderness*, Brené Brown talks about fitting in versus belonging during the quest to find Self. We might interpret these two concepts as being the same thing, but we find profound difference when we stop to consider the terms. When we're chameleons, constantly changing our colours to blend with the people around us or to conform to some preconceived idea of "right," we reinforce our co-dependent mindset. This causes extreme stress and shame, and results in us operating below our capabilities or outside of our values and vision.

When we know who we are and what we have to offer others, we're on our way to finding our inner circle, the people who will love and accept us and actually delight in our quirkiness. I'm reminded of the saying "You're only as good as the company you keep." These are the people we can relax around and grow with. They will become our network and safety net, because they respect our values and won't tolerate our excuses.

Shared Values, Shared Goals

When I became single, some friends didn't fit anymore. Other friends were only available every so often. During and after your divorce, you'll need a larger network of support. We all need to feel connected, to have new and shared experiences, to vent and problem solve by brainstorming with others. Now that you're on this self-improvement path, you'll need to find people who share your values and interests.

In the vein of saying *yes and*, find new hobbies, fitness regimens, and learning opportunities. Look for things to do that offer novel and empowering experiences, and then notice the people who are into these things and the ones you gravitate toward. Finding your inner circle is about finding a social network that includes people who could potentially be life-long friends.

Honour that community as your inner circle. When I talk about finding your inner circle, I'm talking about what happens when we start to do the work on ourselves. When our vibe increases, we start to surround ourselves with people who are vibrating at the same or a higher level. If we're surrounded with healthy and strong people, they become our community. This community is the place to find confidants and mentors.

Our most dramatic upticks in knowledge gathering and personal development come when we engage in aspirational networking. These are your real people, the ones who will challenge you to grow and who will also be challenged by you. If you want to achieve greatness, hang around great people and learn from their modelling.

I'm not suggesting that you shift your dependence to this new group or a person within it. That doesn't help. That would just be co-dependency with a different face.

Looking back on my marriage, I find it interesting that, as co-dependent as I was, I was also a wildly independent person. Lee and I approached our marriage in an independent way. We had different lifestyle preferences and different hobbies and interests. When I think about it objectively, it's no surprise that we're not together anymore. But my point is that I had a number of friends and a social network of my own. I had done a lot of personal work in terms of making sure my inner circle was strong even before it was critical that I do so. When I was separated and going through divorce, not one single person in my most important inner circle surprised me. They showed up as I expected them to and just as they would expect me to if the roles were reversed. That's not necessarily the case for everybody. If you're looking around and not seeing faces of the people you want and need in your life, you've got some housekeeping to do in terms of who you choose to surround yourself with.

My people are the people who are aligned with my value system, people who share my interests, and people who reciprocate. I want to give as much as I get out of an interaction, and I want to feel like the people I'm engaged with are not always taking. Because I tend to be a people pleaser, it's easy for me to fall into lopsided, toxic relationships if I'm not vigorously self-aware.

You probably know what I mean. Most of us have had an emotional vampire or two in our lives. You know, those people who drain our energy, the ones who take, take, take, but when we need them, they don't engage in any meaningful way. They may offer platitudes and toxic positivity advice to make it appear that they care, but are they *doing* anything? Are they really investing in the relationship?

When we start to curate our inner circle, we see people's true colours. It's awesome because it makes us even more grateful for our true friends, and it's empowering because we can make informed decisions about where to put our attention and energy. It's hard, but it's awesome. We give

When our vibe increases, we start to surround ourselves **with people who are vibrating at the same or a higher level.**

ourselves permission to let go of the people who we find ain't our peeps.

But what to do about some of those people who aren't our people but to whom we can't just say "see ya"? Our former in-laws, for example.

Many of the women I work with are shocked not just by being left or being told by a spouse that divorce is the only way, but by how their in-laws treat them and speak about them. If you don't have kids, you're in an excellent position. If you have great relationships with those people and they truly love you, keep 'em. If you don't and they don't, you have *see ya!* freedom. But it's a whole different story if you have children.

Some of us live in the same area as our former in-laws and have younger kids who go to Grandma and Grandpa's. That adds a layer of complexity that we must deal with. I mean, even though there's been a divorce, it's not like we can say, "Okay, these people are no longer in my life." In a way they're a camp. They're not necessarily our camp, but they're part of our children's camp. So, how do we navigate those relationships, and how do we communicate with our kids about all this in ways that reflect our values and model greatness?

First, we must remember that we can't (and shouldn't try to) control other people's behaviour. We can only control the way we interact with them—in this case, with both our in-laws and our kids. That thought helped me determine clear objectives and boundaries.

I thought about it as *you do you, I do me.* I might not always agree with their beliefs and how they manage situations, but I respect their role in my kids' lives and appreciate that they want to stay involved. That's a gift to my children. I just remind myself that I can't take on—as in, play out in my mind or ruminate on—the things that go on in their space.

I hope it's obvious that I'm not talking about ignoring signs of abuse. If you suspect that your children are being willfully abused in any way, please seek qualified professional help.

Of course, none of us are perfect. There are likely going to be times when our kids come back into our home and express hurt or anger about something their father or other mother or one or both of their grandparents said or did. And of course, we're going to have to deal with that in a mature way even if we want to rage or break down and wallow in a pool of our own tears.

I've found that the best way to handle situations like this is to first remember that this has nothing to do with me, and then to lean in with curiosity and support my kids in positive ways by helping them understand what happened, why they feel the way they do about it, and how to move forward. The tricky part is to avoid the temptation to use our children as pawns and to put words in their mouths.

Our kids might come to us and say, "Daddy said..." or "Grandma said..." and it's gonna be about us. And it's gonna Piss. Us. Off. We're going to know damn well that Daddy, other Mommy, Grandma, Grandpa, whoever the hell it was knew damn well that what they did or said was likely to get back to us, and that their motivation was to take a swing at us using the tiny fists of our children, those little people they say they love and want to be their best for. Mama Bear *is* going to rise up in these moments; actually it's often our ego and wounded self with a little *s* rising up and cloaking itself in the skin of a mama bear, because that's socially acceptable. Self-awareness will help us parse our own motives in those moments, and our values will guide what we do next.

It's my belief that, over time, children will form their own opinions about the people in their lives. Doing that for them or trying to influence them is outside the job description of

Mom. I believe that people speak volumes about themselves when they speak about others. So, when faced with negativity in this context, I choose not to engage. I take the higher road. I might say something like, "Well, that's unfortunate that your grandmother speaks that way about me. I have nothing but great things to say about her." I try to leave space for my children's curiosity and gently encourage them to pay attention to the broader picture.

Other comments and questions I've found useful are: "Isn't that interesting? It's unfortunate that was brought up to you. What do you think about it?" And then I ask, "So, how does that play into your values? This is the interesting thing about life. You get to make your own choices and decide how you feel about things like this."

When I get defensive and justify my negative reaction, it shuts down my kids' ability to use rational thought to come to their own conclusions. Kids are very sensitive to the emotional vibes of adults, so I try my best not to manipulate them by revealing strong negative emotions. That's why I have adult friends and an aspirational network. If I need to vent or process, I go to someone I can trust to offer me perspective and guidance and to hold me accountable for my behaviour. If we succumb to a defensive strategy or justification for our anger, all we do is leave our kids with conflicting stories.

Before we move beyond this, I want to make clear that I am not encouraging you to be a doormat or a punching bag. If something their father or someone else has said about me causes my kids to come back and treat me with disrespect or they start throwing accusations at me, I absolutely shut that shit down. If an adult does that to me, if they are being disrespectful, unkind, and standing in judgement, my first thought is *You can quickly go fuck yourself.* I can't and wouldn't say that to my kids, and I can't and won't tell my children that this is an appropriate response when someone disses one of their parents. I must find a way to communicate strong boundaries and my value of being kind always, even when it would be *so* satisfying not to be.

Here's how I respond on my best days: "Listen, there seems to be a lot going on here, and I'm here to help you unpack and work through your emotions and this topic, but I'm not here to be treated with disrespect or to be your punching bag. If you want to talk about this, let's talk. But you're going to treat me fairly, just like you'd want to be treated fairly if it was you. When you're ready to really talk about this and work it all out, let me know." Then I tell them that I love them and want what's best for them, what's truly best, not what might feel the most satisfying in the moment.

Most of our time is going to be spent finding our inner circle, but that's relatively easy compared to navigating the politics of the inner circles we're related to through our children. The thing that gives me comfort and helps me keep a good attitude is that I know I share at least one value with my former husband and in-laws. We all want the children to have as much love and support as we can give—we just may get there a little differently.

Shared Language

When we get divorced, it's not like we switch camps overnight. It's a process, and whether we end up staying in or walking away from what may have been our most intimate camp, during that initial separation and divorce period, the whole inner circle is hurting. Other camp members may be surprised, scared, feeling any number of other emotions and thinking all kinds of thoughts.

During this time, our position in the inner circle changes. We must redefine our role and establish ourselves in a different

People speak volumes about themselves **when they speak about others.**

position. And then we're going to have to teach people how to treat us.

In chapter 6, I talked about how to find your voice and tell people what you need in a broad context. Here, I'm talking about how to do this in a more intimate context, with the people you're going to be around often and for a long time whether you want to or not. This is an opportunity to test the volume and tone of our voice and communicate with others using words they understand and are also willing to use. It's about finding ways to be in agreement or to at least acknowledge each other's perspectives.

Many of the women I talk to don't feel like they have the right to express themselves, especially if they were the ones to initiate the divorce. They look at the pain other people are experiencing and feel shame because they think it's their fault. But that's not fair. Remember: Most of the time, if something's going well it doesn't fail. It might fail if one person can't handle happiness or has some kind of self-sabotaging mindset, but that's rare. It's over. It's not your fault. No, actually, it was part you and part the other person, but blame isn't helpful. It is what it is. Everybody needs to move forward in as healthy a way as possible.

If you find yourself letting people treat or speak to you in abusive ways because you think that the other person is going through a hard time and needs you to cut them some slack, here are a few short responses to keep handy and pull out to say to people when you need to:

- "Okay. I understand that there's more than one way to look at that, but I don't feel the need to explain myself right now because you don't seem like you're in a place to receive it."

- "Listen, I'm practicing [self-care, mindfulness, etc.] right now because I want to be in a better space for myself. I hope you can understand."

- "So, I'm trying to focus on positive things right now and adopt a solution-based mindset. I don't want to gossip or rehash the past, but if you want to have brainstorming session or productive conversation about moving forward, then let's talk about it."

In the worst-case scenario, you might have to say something like this:

- "I'm here to work on our divorce agreement and co-parenting plan. There's no need to speak about any other topic. And when we do speak, it is going to be with respect. It's going to be positive, and it's going to be solutions based as it relates to those two topics."

What's really important is that every time we show up, we show up in this mindset. We take a leadership role. We don't dictate the other person's behaviour or accuse them of being a bad actor, but we do establish how we're going to participate. We lead by example. Trust me when I say that the people around you will start seeing you in a new light. They'll either stick around or run like hell. When you get to this point in your journey, you'll be delighted to find that either choice they make is just fine with you.

Opt In, Opt Out

You should be feeling a sense of pride and self-respect by this point in your growth arc. Heck, I hope you're feeling it right now—like, *Yeah, I got this. Even if nobody else does yet, I know*

*who I am, what I want, and what kind of people I want to hang
with. And I'm starting to see what I do and do not want to do and
who I want to see and not see ever a-freakin-gain.*

People often say to me, "Oh, I know. You just don't have
time. You're so busy." Listen, I'm as busy as I choose to be.
And I'm actually not that busy. I can't always say this out loud,
but when I turn down an invitation or don't volunteer to do
something that others may expect me to do, I'm really saying,
"I choose carefully where I spend my time. That means that
you and I aren't going to see one another until next month.
That doesn't mean I'm busy."

Our society is so hung up on being busy, as if busy is our
default setting and where we're programmed to operate at
our best. It certainly is not, and when we realize this, we start
to make better choices, and communicate those choices.

When we opt out by saying, "No, but thank you," to
someone and they respond, "I know. You're so busy," we can
redirect and test whether a person is on the same frequency
as us by saying, "No, I'm making purposeful choices that help
me honour my body and relationships." Saying that signals
that we're opting out of one thing so we can opt into something more aligned with our priorities. If you receive a deer
in the headlights look, that person isn't your kind of people.
But if the other person says something like, "Oh, I like that.
I'm cutting back too," you know this person might be worth
engaging with.

As you grow, you're going to identify the people you want
to walk away from and the ones you want to walk toward. It's
an audit, edit, like and renew process, with the goal of spending most of your time with the people who are more in line
with your authentic self and your needs. And then it's about
actively seeking out more people. You're going to do that for
a couple of reasons. First, now that you're single, you have

more time on your hands. Second, you're in a difficult season of your life and likely have more needs than your existing inner circle can fulfill.

When I was finding my Self and learning how to be more confident, I strategically aligned myself with the people in my inner circle who I aspired to be like. Old or new. Sometimes I identified someone in my group who was doing something I wanted to do or had a perspective I wanted to learn more about. Other times, I participated in group activities. Either way I was actively reshaping my world and curating the people in it in an effort to maximize my potential. Sometimes I'd find that I didn't have the right people or resources in my life. In those cases I had to fearlessly explore.

Inner Circles, Plural

Just about the time Lee moved out, we had a trip to Vegas on the calendar. The trip was to celebrate a major milestone in the business. I was torn. I wanted to celebrate with the team and to celebrate my part in its success, but I opted out because I knew it would deplete my soul. Sometimes opting out has more to do with the situation, not the people involved.

As it turned out, I immediately had the opportunity to opt into another trip (travel being something I love) with another group. A girlfriend invited me on a ladies-only trip to an all-inclusive resort in Mexico on the same weekend as my originally scheduled trip. *Brilliant*, I thought, and said, "I'm in!" I was vulnerable at the time. I was newly single and thought, *Why not?* The trip would allow me to get out and have some fun and meet new people. Fifty new people as it turned out. That's right—five zero.

No doubt the images running through your mind are the same as the ones that flashed through mine. Knowing my

Sometimes opting out has more to do with the situation, **not the people involved.**

values and knowing what I needed, I told my friend I wanted to go and was quickly embraced with encouragement and compassion to let this experience be whatever I needed it to be with no strings attached.

I booked the flight and, in spite of the group email instructing us to stay together in seats at the back of the plane, I upgraded my ticket and sat closer to the front. Know what you need, and do what's right for you. Check! My self-possessed vibe must have been strong because the guy next to me kept looking over during the flight. His energy was palpable, but I didn't take the bait. I was all *No. Blinders on. I am not here to party. Men are gross to me. I just cannot.*

At one point he turned to me and said, "May I borrow your pen?"

I literally handed him my pen as if it were diseased, infected in some horrible way, and said, "Keep it." I thought, *We don't need to touch. Not even through the pen.*

That didn't dissuade him. "I saw on your form that we're going to the same resort," he went on.

"Oh, really?" Heat rose up my neck and into my hairline. I'm not sure if I was afraid he was hitting on me or if I was ashamed to be going to a singles resort before the ink was dry on my divorce papers.

"Are you going to the meditation retreat?" he asked.

Something about "meditation retreat" made me relax just enough to find my real voice. "Hell no," I said. "I'm with those crazy drunk chicks in the back of the plane."

He laughed and said, "Okay, I feel more accomplished knowing *I'm* going on a meditation retreat."

For the first time since arriving at the airport earlier that day, I was having fun. We ended up talking about all kinds of things. Talking to the gentleman on the plane was serendipitous and started a spark inside of me that changed my life and sticks with me to this day. (I know you're wondering if airplane guy and I hooked up, but I'll leave the kissing and telling for chapter 16.)

The retreat my airplane friend referred to turned out to be a Joe Dispenza event with a group ten times bigger than the group I was travelling with, but their calm energy was one hundred times greater than the loud, live-it-up vibe of my original group. I floated between the two, creating a world of my very own.

I spent most of every day alone, opting out of partying whenever I felt I could without putting a damper on my friend and her friends. I'd often end up in the breakfast line with the meditation retreat participants. On various occasions, different people asked me if I would like a hug. "Yeah... yes," I'd say. "I'd love a hug."

I stayed as open to people and the experiences that felt meaningful to me as I could. I watched what Dispenza's group did and followed suit. I'd wake at the break of dawn and find them doing walking meditations on the beach with the sun and its beautiful morning colours rising out of the ocean. I wondered, *What is this world?* and listened in on discussions about mindfulness and neuroscience. I was hooked.

It was there that I did yoga for the first time. Nobody in the girls' group wanted to do it with me, so I did it by myself. That was okay. I went to a spa for physical touch, emotional healing, and quiet recovery every day until I left. I remember thinking, *Oh my God, this is why people swear by this form of self-care.* I was surrounded by people at the resort but alone most of the time. It was the first time in my life that I didn't feel alone, even when sitting in a dark room or on the beach.

Normally in an environment like that—fifty women drinking and having fun—I'd be all in. The party planner, event coordinator, caregiver, and co-dependent people pleaser would have revelled in and been swallowed whole by all the voices and activity. I would have needed a vacation to recover from my vacation because my default setting was to set my watch by someone else's agenda and match my energy to what I perceived to be their needs. But on this trip, I had the benefit of being in an unfamiliar camp, two unfamiliar camps in fact. I was in the perfect position to ask myself, *What do I want to do? Who do I need to show up and be in this moment? And to which camps do I want to belong?*

One Foot in Front of the Other

For a year and a half, life had thrown everything at me. There had been triumphs and growth for sure, but I felt beaten down and lost. I could have decided to not show up, but deep down, below the pain, I knew my circumstances were the soil of opportunity and fertilizer of greatness. I found my values, my voice, and my needs, and I decided that, from then on, I was going to be a leading lady, not a supporting actress. I opted out of one trip and into another, and I opted out of the experiences there that I knew wouldn't feed me and into those that I sensed would. And, by doing so, I found models for the types of people I wanted in my life and an awareness of another kind of camp I wanted to bring together.

You're part of that. If you're reading this book and feeling beaten down and lost but also hopeful and open, you're where I was on the plane that day. You're probably wondering what's next for you and how you're going to carve out the life you want while going through all the pain and craziness of this post-marriage thing.

Trust me. You're going to do great! When I was living through this in the beginning, all I knew was that I had blind faith. I've always been a spiritual person, but back then I was at the beginnings of my spiritual journey, my shift to mindfulness. But I knew one thing: Put one foot in front of the other in a faithful way, and eventually it will all come together.

8

. . . . .

Dream Big, and Get into Your Next Life

WHEN I was at my lowest, all I had was faith. Sometimes it was a way to passively give up. Other times it was an active surrender to reality. But most of the time it was a feeling of hope that this too shall pass. I was not raised within a formal religion, but I had faith. But the meaning and source of that faith wasn't clear to me.

I wondered where I fell on the spectrum. Was the source of my faith divine, mystic, earthly?

I have come to realize that while faith comes in all shapes and sizes, it always comes from within. Every time I explored this intangible thing called faith, I felt uncomfortable, vulnerable, like an outsider. The more I sat with it, the more I found purpose and belonging on my terms.

At this stage we're experimenting. We're trying things on for size, seeing what fits and what doesn't, and learning to walk in our new skin and on our own two feet. We're starting to see the possibilities, but we're still a bit wobbly. I had self-care fails (still do), yoga fails, and you-name-it fails. And I'm still not sure how to do the church stuff—when to stand, when to sit, how to chant and follow the songs. There were so many things I didn't know but wanted to know, tried to do but couldn't quite stick the landing—*yet*.

That's okay! What matters is that we are beginning to get the sense that we can and will get through this and that we can and will come out on the other side even better. That's faith!

Faith and religion are often described as a practice: the *practice* of faith, the *practice* of religion. Getting up off your knees and then back down on them when you need to. Exercising your voice, off-key at first—sure. But you're using it. You're singing. You're speaking better things into your life and reminding yourself of better things to come. Are you ready to tackle those big, post-divorce projects? Nope. Not yet. But when you finally are finished with this project of divorce, then you'll be able to move on and move up. Home renovation? Yes, after. Start a business? Yes, after. Right now, at this stage, you've got a lot on your plate. You've come a long way, but you've got some rough road and heavy traffic immediately ahead. Now's the time for small but transformative action, and compassion for yourself.

That compassion thing may sound easy, but I struggled so much. Logically I understood that I must truly surrender to the process, to put myself out there, to go through the journey. What was more difficult to connect to, intellectually and emotionally, was the reality that the divorce process takes time and a huge amount of emotional and physical energy. Even though I'd come so far, I still struggled to set realistic expectations for myself and to ignore the expectations placed on me by others.

Expectations Are a Bitch

When I was going through what you're going through now, I thought everything would be wrapped up in short order and I'd be able to get on with my life. But the reality is that the divorce process takes far longer than you might think. You're likely just at the beginning of this highly personal journey. As a coach of women in this phase, I want to keep encouraging you to think of this as a long game. All the stuff we've covered so far regarding personal growth took me three years to discover and muddle my way through. So, settle into the notion of surrendering to the process that is life.

Before I was faced with divorce, which without question has been the biggest challenge of my life, I went through difficult times with the idea of a light at the end of the tunnel. It was a distraction, like a prize. I thought that if I got through the challenge, I would feel a certain way or get a specific thing. But this experience taught me (forced me into?) a new way, a better way. It taught me not to adopt some other seemingly stronger persona and use it to push through the pain for future comfort. Instead, I learned to do things according to my values, my personality, and my authentic self, and to be guided by how I wanted to feel on a consistent basis.

I shifted myself within my world view and reframed my expectations. It's not like, after that, my problems magically went away or I suddenly woke up every day fresh-faced and singing like a Disney princess. I didn't. What I did wake up with was clarity and a sense that I was in control of my destiny.

Did people still judge me? Yes, they did. Are people going to judge you? Yes, they are. But you know what? Fuck 'em. We're authentic (or getting there). We're leading ladies (on most days). We don't judge ourselves (okay, sometimes, but still). We get up every morning with the express purpose of breaking through all the expectations that have held us back. We live to experience the flow of life. We honour our faith by practicing it, and expect good things to come of it when we do.

Expectations can be a bitch, but they can also be a blessing.

Recognize Abundance

The human mind is a wonderful, terrible thing. We can experience the soaring emotions of inspiration while simultaneously feeling stuck. I think that feeling stuck is less about having too few options and more about having so many options that we suffer from analysis paralysis, a sense that with so many unfamiliar choices and so much at stake, we're bound to make the wrong move.

That's fear manifesting itself as reason. That's our lizard brain trying to trick us into not doing anything (staying "safe") by making us think that we're thinking. When we recognize that and acknowledge what's limiting us, we can use that knowledge to get unstuck. Changing my expectations of myself when I feel stuck helps me know how to move through a situation or period more peacefully and easily. The more I gently lean into the feeling, the more rational thought I can apply to it and the more I learn to let go.

Have you ever clasped something so tightly—in your hand, or in your life—that you suffocated it? The same principle applies here. We can't be so afraid of failure and loss that we crush the very thing we want. We can't be so paralyzed with fear that we don't take the first step or the next step or the next on our path to freedom and joy. We can't be so blind to options that we eliminate viable ones.

With more information comes more opportunity for growth. Remember how comfortable you've gotten with change by

*We can't be
so afraid of failure
and loss that*
**we crush the very
thing we want.**

this point and how you're embracing new experiences and learning who you are and what you like and want. Think abundance, not limits. Think about the possibilities, not the problems. This calm before the storm (part III is where we face the real rough stuff) is your opportunity to celebrate your wins and prepare yourself to take everything you've worked to accomplish over the past weeks, months, or even longer to the next level.

This is about your goals becoming more aspirational. This is where you look through the divorce and beyond to the possibilities. But again, we're still firmly in the aspirational right now. This is about adopting a mindset of abundance, not necessarily having abundance. Just learn its name, get to know its face, learn to recognize its voice and its touch.

It took me awhile. Some days were better than others. I could not have imagined how much sticky, icky stuff there was for me to process. In the beginning, I'd be stuck for an entire month processing one feeling or situation. I fought it. I knew I was smart, capable, independent, and strong. I thought that surely I'd quickly make sense of all this and move on. But I could not. Not even a little. I lived in stuck, but I knew better. I recognized that better was waiting for me. I was uncomfortable with stuck. I knew life could be so much more.

When we believe we can do anything, we step up and challenge the status quo. We look for new angles. Letting go of our limiting beliefs, surrendering to the unknown, and loving deeply from within guides us to our connection to Self. This makes our family stronger than ever and provides the best gift to our children.

We hear about and maybe even talk about abundance all the time, but when was the last time you really thought about it? When was the last time you let yourself dream? Dreaming is underrated, so we seldom take time to do it. But when we experience a heartbreaking, knees cut out from underneath of us event, we often hit rock bottom. And it may be cliché, but it's true: When you're at rock bottom, the only place to go is up.

When we allow ourselves to dream big and open our hands and hearts to receive things, we have the courage and energy to climb big mountains and plant our flag at the top— our own damn flag. Making tough decisions and putting yourself out there and embracing the opportunity divorce brings for personal transformation are game changers. It's an opportunity to live any way we choose.

When we accept the gift of the abundance all around us, we understand that it's our right to shine and to shine brightly in the presence of everyone who surrounds us. When we exercise faith, let go of expectations, and recognize abundance, we're planting seeds that, with care and compost, will bear fruit in the future.

Let It Rain

Thinking about all the accusations, rumours, and hurtful actions of your former partner and perhaps even family and community members as fertilizer for the seeds of your dreams can be a powerful coping mechanism. And a reminder: Seeds grow fastest and strongest in darkness and dirt, not in petri dishes or under bright lights. It can be just as helpful to remember that seeds also need water to germinate and grow. So, let your tears flow.

Find a safe place where you can let it all go, but don't be surprised if you're not able to. There have been many times when I could not cry. I had no tears at the times I felt the saddest. I wondered if I'd reached a level of grief beyond sadness and if I was experiencing the numbness of despair and

Our safe spaces aren't the places where **we bear fruit.**

hopelessness. That was almost as scary as the fear of breaking down in tears at inopportune times: at a PTA meeting, in the check-out line at the grocery store, or maybe even in front of Lee on a day when he seemed not to have a care in the world.

At those times, I would sometimes feel the urge to cry so strongly that my throat would clench. I would choke on my breath, but no tears would flow. I'd try to distract myself any way I could. I discovered that if I had a few drinks, I'd often become emotional, and the tears could flow. So, as I stepped away from habits like drinking that could, tears or no tears, take me nowhere fast, I had to find a solution.

Unfortunately, I didn't feel like I had a safe place to let go. Sometimes I couldn't let the tears flow. Other times I didn't feel like I should. If I let go, I thought, I might crumble and never return. I was afraid my kids might walk into my room or walk by me as I was bent over the kitchen sink. I was afraid they would see me and be afraid or sad. As I staggered about town trying to keep my routine and hold myself together, I wondered if strangers could see my tearless, puffy eyes through my sunglasses.

My commitment to my self-care routine may have saved me. I discovered the safety and solitude of the beach, walking in nature, and conversing with the wind. I found a safe space in the privacy of my car and permission in sad music. I found release on my yoga mat and in the pages of my journal. When I couldn't let the tears flow at home, I knew I had a place to go later to let it all out.

Our safe spaces aren't the places where we bear fruit. They are the places where we heal, the places we allow our tears to cleanse our minds and soothe our hearts. They are the places we honour our bodies and use the outpouring of them to nurture the seeds of our future.

Life Runs in Parallel

You're going to be growing and experiencing small and big wins in your personal life—the life inside you. But you're also going to experience low lows. The growing peace in your interior life is likely not going to manifest in your external life, the life that requires you to interact with your former spouse and find a new normal. So, don't let this process take longer than it has to, or let it negatively affect you any more than it must.

Let your aspirations pull you toward your next life. Dream big and have the courage to go for the next thing. But you know as well as I do that the next big thing—all those gut-wrenching firsts—is what's coming up. Remember that compost I mentioned a page or so back? Well, that was a nice way of saying *shit*. We're about to step into the shit. It stinks. It's not fun, but there's no way around it. The good news is that there's power in poop if we dream big by planting good seeds in the prepared soil of our new mindset. We can know that, in the end, that compost is the very thing that will allow our hopes and dreams to bear the fruit that will sustain us for the rest of our lives.

Remember who you are and what you want, and when pressure comes that tempts you to conform to someone else's ideal, stay strong and be you. Don't get stuck in the past or too distracted by present pain. Dream big. Keep up your practices and keep the faith. Maintain your momentum.

three

FIRSTS ARE GOING **TO HIT YOU HARD**

9

. . . . .

Sharing
the News

NOTHING MAKES a pending divorce real like announcing it. How do you even do it? So much time and energy goes into just thinking about it. Our brain sifts through countless ways of positioning things, "right" ways and "wrong" ways and any number of potential reactions ranging from supportive to downright embarrassing and horrible. It's exhausting, but it's part of the process. And there's no getting around this part, so you might as well get through it as quickly and graciously as possible. And, hey, it might not be as bad as you think it'll be. On the other hand, it might be worse. There's no way of knowing until you do it.

Think about all the things you've anticipated in your life—first sexual encounter, first day at a new job, first childbirth. A while back my daughter tried bubble gum for the first time. She'd been waiting all her life, for six whole years, to try it. Her excitement was palpable and contagious. After a few short minutes, reality set in. The flavour was gone. The thrill was gone. All that anticipation and energy for three seconds of pleasure.

That's life. We anticipate the pleasure or pain of so many things. We build the experience up in our heads only to find that the reality is never what we expected. Things we think will be great often turn out to be nothings, and things we think are going to be unbearable often go exceedingly well. Most of the time, they fall somewhere between those poles, and this chapter is all about helping you get through those difficult firsts, so you can ultimately move on to the fun ones.

In October 2015, two months after Lee's eyes said, "It's over," we decided to tell our children that we were getting a divorce. Our oldest was five, and our youngest was one. We told the kids first, then our parents, and then I hopped on a plane to share this news with my brother. We then told our closest friends and asked that they, our inner circle, share the news at their discretion with as many people as they felt reasonable. That was a risky move but one that relieved some of the burden and allowed us to focus on our children during a critical time.

We made the decision to announce our impending divorce in October because we looked ahead to what was coming—school starting, Thanksgiving, Christmas, and so on—and saw an opportunity to model greatness. We wanted to control the timing and teach people how to deal with the situation by being purposeful.

Anticipate and Plan

Lee and I decided to officially separate that month, but we still lived under the same roof and gradually uncoupled to give ourselves and our kids time to adjust and make necessary arrangements. We didn't physically separate until June. I don't know which way is harder: ripping the bandage off or doing it like we did. In the beginning, working together as co-parents and trying to be smart and gracious was so hard. I would have preferred to climb into a hole and never come out, but I believe that, all things considered, we did make the best decision for our family.

Even though we were living together, I was on my own. I was learning how to navigate through time and space largely by myself. For most of the things I shared in parts I and II, I was going through them alone but next to Lee. It was weird and hard. There were so many little firsts and so many big firsts to come. It was difficult not to get overwhelmed. I mean, we can only take so much.

So, I learned to face it all and find a way to anticipate these firsts so I could be ahead of them emotionally, instead of reacting to and being exhausted by them every time. Life can feel like death by a thousand papercuts if we let it. Anticipating what's coming and planning for it at least gives us some level of control, even if the result we imagine is off in some way.

The pressure of sharing the news is difficult. You may not have the luxury of talking it through with your spouse and making decisions that are in your and your family's best interests. And if you can discuss it with your spouse and craft your announcement together, you'll both be coming into the conversation with different perspectives and experiences. Even so, you have to find a way to communicate the news to others in a way that reflects your shared experience and that is productive rather than destructive.

Most women I talk to (because they're the proactive type, as evidenced by them seeking legitimate help) feel their partner is not an active participant at the table. My heart goes out to those of you who must deliver the news completely on your own. Many of my clients express frustrations like, "Are you kidding me? Not only is this not my choice, not only have I been trying for years, but now I've got to go saddle up during a vulnerable time and take the entire leadership role for this divorce as well? I'm tired already!" But no surprise, right? You're taking the load again. That's what you've done your whole marriage. And that's what you're going to do again. Yes, there's a certain amount of anger attached to having to take the lead, but there's also a certain amount of self-respect. If we look at it that way, it can drive us to do things in a way that supports our long-term goals. We can use the poor modelling we see as a guide for what not to do.

When I was considering what was to come, all I felt was shame and guilt. I imagined and experienced a tremendous amount of judgement, and I didn't want to face that from my family, friends, or peer groups. I felt the pressure of being the first person in my entire family to get a divorce. I'd never directly watched anyone walk through the process, much less do so in a way I'd want to emulate. We had to make it up as we went.

One night, Lee and I sat at the dinner table and discussed how we were going to position things and when and how we'd tell each group of people.

Like I said, it was not my choice to end the marriage. But after a while I'd come to realize that I was an equal participant and had played an equal role in our marriage coming to that end. For me to take ownership of that was a huge step in my personal growth, and I know I wouldn't have come through this ordeal as well as I have had I not reached that place.

Now, it's not like I was happy or didn't still sometimes listen to that little voice that whispered, "It's not your fault. It's all him. He's the bad guy. He ended it. This isn't your choice. You're the victim here." This is a common struggle. Many of my clients and workshop participants have a hard time stepping into the ownership space. If you're facing having to

If we want to be in a space to cooperate with our former partner, we first have **to have a healing of the mind.**

make an announcement, you're probably feeling what I was at that time—resentment, anger, sadness that your marriage is ending, and thoughts of what to blame in order to be vindicated. These things are natural and you're allowed to feel them, but your thinking brain is probably telling you that you did play some part in this and it's not going to do any good to throw anyone under the bus.

One of the things that kept me from giving into my fear and anger was to think ahead and imagine how my attitude and words would influence the people who would be regularly interacting with my children. It was heart-wrenching to think about how I'd feel if it ever got back to me that someone had said something to make my kids think their daddy is a bad guy. So, for me, it was about finding a way to communicate the facts with integrity, in a way that wasn't dishonest but that could still have a positive influence on future outcomes. That can be a very fine line.

When I delivered the news to those closest to me, I kept it simple. I told them that Lee and I had decided to separate and were going to divorce. I specifically said, "We're moving forward with a lot of respect for our family, and we're focusing on what's best for the children." I left it at that with every single person. There were probably only three people in the world who knew the full story from my perspective, and one of them was my therapist. The more you say and the more people you say it to, the more opportunity there is for misinterpretation and for unflattering things to work their way back to you and your children. As we discussed in chapter 6, it's just not worth the risk.

When we choose to be deliberate communicators and to act from a place of values-based intent when faced with all these firsts, we come away with a sense of empowerment as opposed to racing through them with blinders on and learning nothing. At the end of the day, you're not so much working through a problem as you are working on you, so that you can transform and become your authentic self. Not only will you benefit, so will everyone you engage with.

Sharing the News with Your Kids

If there's one thing that every parent going through a divorce gets hung up on, it's how to tell their children. If you're a parent, you've probably thought, *Oh my God, this is going to crush them.*

This is a good time to step back and remind yourself of your values, how you want to feel, and how you want to make others feel. Do you value family, your kids in particular? Do you want to be a coach and to mentor them through this? This process is an opportunity to help your children discover things about their own values and needs and to learn what works best for them as you all grieve and grow. Kids, especially young kids, take their cues from the people around them.

And truthfully, in terms of sharing the news and going into this new space, I think the message you share with your larger family is the same one you share with your kids, because you are teaching that family how to engage with your children when you are not around—they are also gatekeepers of your children's emotional well-being and you want to make sure you give them your vision and protocol. Keep the message clear, concise, and age and stage appropriate. Kids don't need to know all the details. "The talk" can be as simple as: "Mommy and Daddy are going to be going from married to being friends. Friends live in different houses, but they still love each other and share things, just like Mommy and Daddy are going to share time with you. Mommy will always be your Mommy, and Daddy will always be your Daddy.

*What matters most
to kids is stability.
Divorce in
and of itself does
not hurt kids.*
Conflict does.

Our love for you will never change." If your kids are a little older, you might say, "You know what? We are going to be figuring out a lot of things as a family. What we guarantee is that we will always be transparent and inclusive as we work through what we all need as we understand our new family dynamic." Presenting a united, emotionally neutral front sets many children at ease. You might even be surprised when a little one jumps up and says, "Okay, can I go watch *Dora the Explorer* now?"

Whether they grasp it at first and regardless of whether it upsets them, you're setting the tone and including them in the discussion. You're helping your kids have a sense of control and input. Perhaps the most important part in all of this, whether you communicate it explicitly or let the subtext speak, is that your divorce has nothing to do with the kids. It's going to impact them. They're going to be part of it, but it's not their fault. And they certainly don't need to take on any responsibility for solving problems or propping up the ego or emotions of either parent.

One of the things I help clients remember is that each child is an individual. You could have four kids all in similar ages and stages, but each one might need radically different help and connections through the process. This is where I go back to the idea that this thing's too big to go through alone. In those early days, when I relied on a licensed therapist to help me through, I set up one session for myself and the next session for my kids. It's important that we have some professional guidance, even if it's in the form of easy-to-access self-help tools and books like this, created by people who have experienced it themselves and have come out on the other side happier and healthier. There are a lot of resources for kids out there. One child may benefit from art therapy, another by journalling or getting involved in an extracurricular activity.

I want to acknowledge that I'm coming from a place of privilege in this regard. My children's father is a loving, supportive dad who worked with me to break the news to our children. I also live in Canada where there is more support for women than in other countries, and I was in a position to work with a professional therapist. Some of you may have been rolling your eyes or swallowing your tears reading this because it's a reminder of the support you don't have and the love your children aren't going to get from their other parent. I wish I could wrap my arms around you right now and let you cry on my shoulder and help you know that you and your children are not alone.

The best thing I can do is to encourage you to communicate your situation and values as best you can to your precious children, and remember that if you've been in a bad situation, your kids probably already know. They likely understand what's been going on because they've been experiencing what you've been experiencing over the years, so it's really not a shock to them (and probably won't be to your family and friends either).

No matter who you are or what your situation is, it's also important to remember that you don't have to have all the answers. Just because you're a mom doesn't mean you know everything and can or should answer everything. Even now when my kids come to me with questions, I sometimes can only say, "Honey, relationships are complicated. They have a lot of moving parts. Nobody enters a marriage thinking that they're going to end it. In time, when you can understand more about relationships, we'll talk about that." Sometimes I have to say, "That's an interesting question. I'm actually not sure of the answer, but I'll get back to you if you give me time to think about it."

We don't have to be perfect. We just have to tell our kids what's going on. What matters most to kids is stability. Divorce in and of itself does not hurt kids. Conflict does.

Sharing the News with Family and Friends

Telling our kids we're getting divorced is one thing. But let's be honest: There's a lot of to-ing and fro-ing and being in limbo until we make things public. It's kind of like how you're not officially in a relationship until you update your Facebook status.

To be clear, I'm not recommending that you use Facebook or any other social media platform to announce your split. I mention Facebook tongue-in-cheek, but how and when we tell the outside world matters. I recommend taking the same approach you've been practicing since chapter 6 and that you used when you shared the news with your kids. Keep things simple, and don't give in to the temptation to vent.

As hard as it might be at times, we must always take the high road.

The high road is easy to find and stay on when we know our values and goals, and when we map out a way to communicate those in a straightforward way. Give people enough information to know what's happening but not so much that it opens the door to a game of twenty questions or allows you to start justifying, defending, and losing your integrity.

Telling our family members was fairly straightforward. I felt the guilt and shame but told it like it was. Telling friends was harder in some ways. I guess because we have this sense that, no matter what, our family will always be there. They'll get over it or bury their feelings under a rug and things will equalize. That's not necessarily the case with friends, especially couple friends.

All of our friends were married. We socialized as couples. Although some were in second marriages, everyone was coupled up. Our divorce would upset the entire group dynamic. Marriage was a thing, a status. And as we got closer and closer to telling people, phrases like "broken home" played and replayed in my mind. I wanted to take ownership of my part, but I didn't want to own that. And people can get quite judgey when you tell them about what many view as a personal failure at best and a sin against God at worst. I had to actively remind myself that I wasn't bound to other people's language and beliefs and that I had the power to redirect them if I wanted to.

The thing I was aware of and anticipated was that they were going to start their own grieving process. I wouldn't be able to bear that burden for them or protect them from it. Divorce has a domino effect. I knew that the moment I shared this news, ready or not, they were going to have to take it in and process it. Keeping that in the front of my mind helped me craft language and speak in a tone that was understanding and open.

That mindset and presentation helped; I have no doubt. Most of our family members and friends were great and offered support. When we gave them permission to selectively pass the word along to others, we asked them to follow our lead and keep things short and sweet. I really was still in victim/martyr mode. But I knew that wasn't the true story, and I didn't want it to become my story. So, I didn't tell it. I kept silent and let others who weren't as emotionally attached handle things.

Doing these things—or not doing these things—allowed me to protect my authentic self, as fragile as it was. It allowed me to protect my children, and it allowed me to protect my energy.

People can't reshape truth and share stories if they have **no information to work with.**

Were people talking behind my back? Gossiping about my situation? If they were, I didn't hear about it. Frankly, I didn't care. My position is this: People are free to discuss and carry on as they will. They'll tell whatever stories they want, stories that support their insecurities and provide an excuse for their anger. Gossip can be a diversion, a distraction from the problems that people see but don't want to acknowledge in their own lives. We can't worry about that. We've got enough on our plates.

Shut the Door on the Rumour Mill

We've talked about the temptation to overshare and people's propensity to dig for dirt and pass it along, but it bears repeating here because you're going to feel very vulnerable at this critical point. You've lost your primary support system and a person whose arms you could fall into during hard times. You're going to be hungry for love and at the same time ready to rage.

It's easy to get lured in by a seemingly understanding friend or associate. It's not like life stops so we can do the whole divorce thing and emerge reformed and beautiful on the other side. While all this divorce drama is going on, it's overlapping with real life. We go to social events and stay connected to friends. That puts us in the path of gossips and those people who, kind of like the prayer chain at church, don't really care about us but do care about the juicy info they can gather and use for their own purposes.

This is why, when you understand your values and set boundaries, you have to be the one to protect them every single time someone crosses them. I decided that I would always speak with positivity and respect. I would not share details. These were my boundaries. I kept my answers short, sweet, and truthful. When someone pressed for more information, I'd pull out my pre-determined response: "This is certainly the most challenging time I've ever been through, but we're working through it. We have a lot of love, respect, and friendship, and we're focusing on the children."

Some of us feel an obligation to share when people are being kind or to provide details when asked a question, but we don't owe anyone anything. And it can be really hard if you're a classic Type A like me, someone whose brain is always whirling and has a gazillion stories happening at once up in there. I always give answers. I give solutions. I give opinions on the fly. I realized this in the beginning and recognized that while it's a strength in some ways, it could hurt me in others. Sometimes we just need to shut that stuff down in our own minds, and also when other people start to engage us in ways that go too far—because those behaviours can reinforce our co-dependent leanings and lead us to share information we shouldn't with people we shouldn't.

The bottom line is that, outside of full-blown lying, people can't reshape truth and share stories if they have no information to work with.

Outside and In

I can't overemphasize the importance of a dual approach— doing the interior work of changing our mindset and the exterior work of changing the way we communicate and interact with people. Because if we want to be in a space to cooperate with our former partner, we first have to have a healing of the mind, and to purposefully carve out space for ourselves to practice mindfulness and stillness. We're not going to be able to focus on supporting our kids. We're not going to have the mental strength and emotional fortitude to do some of these other things that are coming up.

Even if you have the benefit of a spouse who's willing to sit down with you and plan and who will invest the time and emotional energy in delivering the news with you in a respectful way, the tough part really isn't sharing the news. We get caught up in the anxiety of this devastating moment, but the tough stuff actually happens in the days and years after we update our official status and tell the world, "It's over."

10

·····

Move Out Day

OVER MONTHS of living together but separated from Lee, I'd faced many small firsts. It felt like that old standard: one step forward and two steps back. Yes, I was always making progress, but the setbacks left me feeling like I would never gain traction. And the biggest setback came in June 2016.

I'd anticipated this milestone first. I'd walked through the day in my mind and through what I imagined the space would look like after he was gone. My irrational fear of death and dying rushed at me head on. I saw the empty seat at the table. I saw his side of the closet, empty. It felt to me like the day he would die and never return to the home we'd shared and the family we'd made, but I was powerless to stop it. All I could do was determine what I needed out of that day, how I'd move forward.

The first thing I knew was that I didn't want to be at home. I couldn't watch his things go out the door even though Lee had hired a moving crew to do the work and wouldn't be on site that day. I sent the children away for the night, so I could come back and clean the home before they returned. It needed to be cleaned, organized, and put back together. Or maybe I needed to spend time cleaning it and use that work to purge through my sadness and anger—this was also the day the family pictures came down. I knew I'd need time to settle my emotions. So, I left the home of what was and prepared myself to step into the house that would be.

Knowing that Lee had hired movers, I decided one other thing. No matter what shape I found the house in, I wouldn't take it personally. That didn't make stepping back into the house any easier. What I found did and didn't surprise me.

The movers had removed everything Lee valued and left everything else behind.

As agreed, he hadn't taken any furniture. He hadn't wanted it. He wanted his clothes and some gym stuff and the wine cellar. Yes, it was more his collection than mine, but I still felt the sting. When I opened his closet, all the good clothes were gone, with some leftover pieces lying around. Elsewhere, I found discarded odds and sods, stupid things like protein shakes and artwork that had been his.

Fury welled inside me.

I thought, *Well, isn't this hunky fucking dory? You go to a brand-new snazzy house, start completely fresh in a beautifully decorated, well-appointed space, you take all the best wine, and your hired muscle just leaves what's left—what's not good enough for your new life—on the floor of mine!*

I had taken on the role of jealous victim and martyr and was playing it out beautifully in my mind. I wanted to murder, but I channelled that devastating sadness into productivity.

Channel Your Pain

Pain can be an amazing motivator. I grabbed a trash bag and went through the house room by room. I got rid of everything left over that was his. I went through the bar and pared back the liquors and drink ingredients. Gone were his favourites. What remained were mine. I looked at everything of mine and got rid of any old things that weren't serving me anymore. Gone. So much stuff, gone.

When I got to the closet, I scooped up all his leftovers, shoved them into a bag, and then filled his side with my stuff. I decorated shelves. I hung some inspirational items on the wall. I rearranged the double vanity area, creating a make-up station on one side and a hygiene station on the other. I made that space my own. I took control in the moment and considered my options. I could stay there and focus on the empty spaces and what was lost, I could love where I lived and make it my own, or I could find a new house and start fresh.

That thought gave me pause. I was intentional and deliberate in my analysis. At first, I wanted to run. I would have run to a different continent if I could have, but I have kids so I didn't. Then I thought I could move to Toronto. That would have been complicated, so I decided to stay in the area. Over the course of the next few months, I looked at real estate. In the end, I decided that, with him moving out, there had already been a massive change. Move or no move, things will be different. I realized that living within new bricks and mortar wasn't going to ease my grief.

We can move from one place to another, but everything we carry inside moves with us.

I've always believed that it's unwise to make big decisions in moments of crisis, so I chose to hold my ground and live in a space of discomfort. I chose to heal through it rather than run from it. The last thing I did that night was take down the family pictures. Doing the other cleanup and rearranging had helped calm my emotions. Taking those images off the walls, bookshelves, and tables made it all too real. He was gone.

Recently, someone asked me if I thought about my children in that moment, if I was afraid that taking the pictures of their dad down would make them feel like I was trying to wipe him away, sanitizing him out of their lives. Honestly, I didn't. Rage overcame me again. I couldn't let those photos stay.

The Realities of This New Normal

I've since included my kids in every possible decision, whether it's major or just cosmetic. I say things like, "Hey guys, what do you think about this?" or "Hey, Mommy's going to do [fill in the blank]. I'm running this by you. Is there anything you'd like to add to it?"

Thankfully, my kids were so young when their dad moved out that they didn't notice a lot. Many of the things I removed had started to blend into the clutter, so they didn't miss them. They noticed the big things, like one car in the garage where there used to be three. That was one of their big deal moments.

What seemed to matter most to my children was staying in their family home. To this day, I don't think they care what changes I make to our space as long as it's their family home. It's the place itself they're attached to, not so much what it looks like on the inside. Having said this, I knew it would be important to give them something to look forward to, and I now recommend this to clients with kids at any age.

When they got home the next day, I hugged them and said, "Hey, you get to have two bedrooms now, one with Mommy and one with Daddy. How do you want to decorate your spaces?" They were excited about that. So they redecorated their room and that was their way of changing their space and starting over like their dad and I did. For the most part, it was a lot of little changes that amounted to major shifts in how we emotionally and physically lived in the space.

We can move from one place to another, **but everything we carry inside moves with us.**

Eventually, we got rid of the dinette table too. Without Lee at it, I hated that table. If you have kids, you know how much time they spend around the dining room table, especially when they're young—breakfast, lunch, dinner, snack, and crafts. It's their home base. Interacting with them at that table made me acutely lonely. I found myself barking at them about their manners and anything else that was even remotely related to what they were doing as they sat there. That wasn't working for them or me. That table kept us anchored in the past when we needed to move forward and find our own flow.

Part of finding flow is creating ways of keeping your kids in the loop about what will happen on a day-to-day basis. Whether you have full or joint custody, the reality is that you just cannot do everything, and the more we can include our children in the planning and doing of tasks, the more we reduce their anxiety.

Calendars worked to keep us organized and prepared for what was coming up. We hung them and clearly marked Mommy Days and Daddy Days. I asked them how they wanted to approach transition days—if they wanted family time (play games, watch a movie, or something else) before they left, and if they wanted the same love buffer when they came home. We talked about what they wanted to take to their dad's and the need to collect that stuff up so it was ready when it needed to be. My daughter suggested we make a checklist. "Great idea, honey." So, we made a checklist. We decided we needed a couple of baskets by their doors—a place where anything going between homes could land—so we got those. A lot was changing, but a lot of it was fun for them. They got to pretend to be grown-ups.

I also said, "Okay, now I need you to help me cook and take out the garbage and set and clear the table." It's amazing what kids will do when we present things to them in a positive way and show them that we need them just as much as they need us. As we worked on projects together, I saw that the kids were starting to take on a sense of pride and ownership. Four became three, but those three got real tight.

I signed official divorce papers a month after Lee moved out. The lead-up time to our physical separation was slow. But when it all came down, it came down fast and hard.

I'm glad I chose to stay in our family home because it's true: Home *is* where the heart is. But my children had two homes now, and a mommy's heart always beats with her children's.

11

. . . . . .

The First Transition Day with Your Kids

I N THE first days and weeks after the physical separation, don't be surprised if you find yourself in limbo. Your routine will be thrown completely out of whack, and your emotions will likely vacillate anywhere from optimism to relief to despair. And in all that, you've got to prepare for and get through the experience of doing the kid hand-off with your former partner.

Before our first hand-off, the kids and I talked and worked out the plan. I'd been smiley and positive, telling the kids they were going to have a great time with Daddy. I actually thought that maybe we'd get through this okay. Or at least that the kids would.

When Lee's car pulled into the driveway, both kids started crying. My daughter had a full-on crying attack and wailed that she didn't want to leave her mommy. My son clung to my neck and sobbed like only a toddler can. "No, no. It's fine. This is going to be fun. You love Daddy, and he's excited to see you. It's okay. Daddy's gonna bring you back tomorrow.

It's just one night," I said. Honestly, I can't believe I was able to speak.

As I tried to get the kids into the car, my son clutched my neck and kicked and screamed and braced his feet against the door to prevent me from putting him into the car. On the inside, I was having a meltdown of my own. My babies were hurting, and my mind went to all the places I'd worked so hard not to let it and other people's go:

This decision has crippled them.

They absolutely are from a broken home no matter what you try to tell yourself.

This is going to psychologically impact them for years to come. And *This is it. I've ruined my children.*

And then *Oh my God, what am I going to do without my children? I've never been without them.*

I finally got them into the car and waved and smiled and blew kisses as the car drove away. I'd willed myself to do what I'd pre-determined to do that day, and then I carefully walked back into the house. I turned and closed the door slowly, locked the bolt, and folded to my knees. Within a few seconds, I was lying on the floor weeping uncontrollably. It was as if my heart had struck the floor and been broken in two. That moment took me right back to the visceral beginning.

Seeing that car go down the road made me feel like I was being pruned from my family, like I'd been surgically removed.

It's hard to prepare for the ebb and flow of emotions at this time. Sometimes we prepare for a strong reaction to something, but that reaction doesn't come. At other times, we think nothing of something and are suddenly hit with a deluge of grief. I learned to cope during this time by practicing what I shared in parts I and II, but there were sometimes weeks at a stretch when I was pretty useless.

Practice Compassion but Play It Safe

In hindsight, I think that, whenever possible, we should go through these things as a family because it can give us perspective. I do think it's true that moms often bear the emotional burden in heterosexual relationships while dads stand back and don't get as emotionally involved with their kids. But even in the midst of all my emotional pain and attention to getting them into their dad's car that first transition day, I was aware of Lee.

He looked absolutely gutted. I can only imagine what he was thinking, but it must have been something like, *Oh my God, my children don't even want to come with me.* They were crushed, I was crushed, and he seemed crushed too, but he had to take the kids. It's not easy for anyone. In the midst of my pain, I felt compassion for him. He hadn't called our marriage off out of spite or from a place of neglect. He'd been hurting. That was his reality, and divorce was the only way he saw to escape that pain and move toward a destination of his choosing.

As I learned to look at Lee through a lens of compassion, my rage went away. I started to process my thoughts and emotions in healthy ways. I was able to focus on helping him be a good co-parent because, when the kids are with him, he needs to be their go-to person. As tempting as it sometimes is to want him to fail and be the bad guy, I really do want him to succeed. I really do want transition days to be fun and respectful.

The assumption might be that everyone in a divorce is hurting and that the other person is a decent human being at their core. Unfortunately, the reality is that many of you are dealing with a narcissistic or perhaps even an abusive person. The reality is also that the break-up stage of a relationship is

Most of the time,
whatever your former
partner is doing has
nothing to do with you.
**It's their problem,
their pain.**

the most dangerous time in a woman's life. Some of you may rightly fear for your safety and feel frustrated by idealized situations or advice that assumes that all actors are rational and seeking what's best for the children involved.

You might be wondering how to balance compassion and safety. As far as I'm concerned, that's a line in the sand. If you're concerned about safety, you need to put that first. Figure out how to feel safe first and let compassion come later. You might meet in a neutral place and have witnesses assist with the hand-off. I have several clients whose relationship with the other person is so strained that they aren't permitted to communicate via text, email, or phone. They use an app that's monitored by professionals. Your attorney, local law enforcement agencies, and women's shelters can tell you what your options are and assist in getting you the help and protection you need.

Regardless of your situation, compassion isn't as much for the other person as it is for ourselves. It helps us see and acknowledge the pain in other people's lives. It helps us do that for ourselves too. It doesn't excuse our bad behaviour or anybody else's. It speaks to our values and allows us to get closer to our authentic selves and model greatness for our children and others who look to us for leadership.

This Is a Test

Let's stay with this idea of narcissism for bit longer because it comes up all the time. We throw the word around these days and tend to label anyone who exhibits any selfishness or lack of awareness as a narcissist. Let's be honest and acknowledge that by doing this, we're diagnosing others from a place of ignorance. Trained mental health professionals—at least the ones who adhere to strict ethical standards—do not diagnose mental illnesses without personally engaging with a patient.

Beyond that, the diagnosis is protected by doctor-patient confidentiality.

As laypeople and injured parties, we are wholly unqualified to make that assessment. And if we subscribe to the idea that nobody has a right to label us or tell a version of our story that we don't authorize, it's hard to defend the idea of labelling someone else a narcissist.

Having said that, I do think we should be bold in identifying narcissist*ic* behaviour and why it bothers us so much. If we focus on why it bothers or damages us rather than on the person doing the behaviour, it will often point us to a value or preference we didn't know we had. When a client comes to me to point out their former partner's actions and labels that person a narcissist, I say, "Listen, the more that you focus on all of his defects and all of his flaws and keep this gerbil on the wheel going round and round, the more you play a part in it."

The better thing for us to do in these situations is to consider why we're attracted to that type of person and drama, so we can stop that cycle. Let's face it, second marriages have an even higher likelihood of ending in divorce than firsts, so we need to get back in our lane and start driving on the right side of the road. If we don't, we're going to run into the same type of nonsense again and again.

I find that the best way for me to stay in my lane is to exercise compassion, which ultimately leads to forgiveness. A lot of us struggle with the idea of forgiveness. And of course we do, because for many reasons we find it difficult to forgive ourselves when we don't live up to our own standards. So much of this book—this journey—is about unpacking that stuff and leaving it on the side of the trail. I mean really. We've got to let that shit go. We've got to let that other person go.

Most of the time, whatever your former partner is doing has nothing to do with you. It's their problem, their pain. It's not personal. Or, I should say, it's not about us. And when it is, we go back to our values and boundaries. We see what's happening as an opportunity to practice what we've learned so far and figure out what we've mastered and what we need to put more thought and energy into.

Mindset. Ownership. Growth. Leadership. Resiliency. These are the things that matter and that we can pass on to our kids. They are also all predicated on awareness, an in-the-moment assessment of what's happening and what our next step needs to be. I often hear (as I'm sure you do) people say, "I'm stuck in the past," and then express a sense of missing out on something. I get it. I've been there. It's as if we believe that if we look hard enough at the past, we'll discover that missing thing. But that's rarely what happens.

And then there's the flip side—always looking to the distant future as a distraction, a daydream that keeps our heads out of the moment our bodies are actually in. This makes sense too. We want to look at things that make sense to us, and we're looking for ways to control the narrative about anything even remotely uncomfortable.

But if we require ourselves to stay in the moment and rationally reframe our thinking about it, life becomes pretty darn good. Even the move out day. Even transition days. We have the power to anticipate and reframe all these firsts. They can be anything we want them to be. Whether you're going through the worst of it or the best of it, all that matters is what it is to you.

Let Go and Look Ahead

These days are going to happen either way. We might as well let go of the past, walk through each moment with as much grace as we can, and look to the future that is truly within our reach—a future of healthy independence and one that includes healthy interdependent relationships.

When we let go of the past, we free our hands to reach for the next most accessible thing. For some people, that's a feeling of safety. For other people, it's joy. The next most accessible thing, remember, is an action that leads to a feeling. We're stepping out in faith to do this thing—whatever that thing is for you—so we can feel a certain way. These are productive things that starve fear and feed our authentic selves. Each small win builds momentum, making the next big first easier even when it would be challenging under the best of circumstances.

12

· · · · ·

The Flip Side of Traditions

REGARDLESS OF what time of year you and your partner separate, there's likely a holiday just around the corner. If you have kids, Thanksgiving and Christmas might be the worst for you. Whether you have kids or not, Valentine's Day is likely to feel like you've been stabbed in the heart.

Even if for the most part you maintain previous rituals (trick-or-treating on Halloween, all the same foods on Thanksgiving, new jammies and hot cocoa on Christmas Eve, chocolates and love notes on Valentine's), it's still going to be different. We can feel a great deal of loneliness even when our children are around because we're likely to fantasize about the past and what family looks like. We can fall back into that "broken home" mind trap because we've been conditioned to think that family means nuclear or conjugal family, two parents and their kids. We might still be mourning the loss of that, and having to do it while celebrating special occasions with our kids.

Some kids, especially older ones, will be acutely aware of the absence of their other parent and will be mourning too. So, it's important to stay aware of our children's needs and preferences and keep them involved in decision making. As always, it helps to think ahead to what has the potential to activate us and find healthy ways to self-soothe.

One of the things that helped me was to reframe my idea of family. This is becoming easier and easier as society changes. The idea of chosen family, a group of people we love but who we aren't related to by blood, is gaining traction. I love this. It allows me to gather people around me and create new traditions. As an extrovert I love to entertain, and I find these gatherings comforting.

Your Place, Your Party

In my world, nothing's a party like a dinner party. So, I stepped back into hostess mode as often as I could. Before, Lee and I had this whole dance. He chose the music playlist and served the drinks. I created the menu and took care of food service. I was on social detail and loved every second of it. And when everyone had gone home, we did clean up a certain way.

After the divorce I was flying solo, but I still tried to do all the things. It was exhausting! I really thought that I needed to maintain the elements of my parties that people had enjoyed from "the old days." In some ways, I think I twisted past expressions of enjoyment into expressions of expectations for how things should always be. After a few tries, my thinking brain bitch-slapped that lizard brain and educated it about my highest vales and how we really wanted to feel. I want to offer my home to my guests. I want them to come and be with me, me as my Self. What I'd been doing, though, was attempting a Jedi mind trick to make my guests see things as they'd been when Lee and I were together. I was trying to distract from his absence by filling it myself. That just doesn't work. We only have one body with one set of hands and a finite amount of creativity and energy.

I'd already gone through the house and redecorated. It was my pictures hanging on the wall, my colours, my area rugs, my plants. My mindfulness and Oracle cards were on the tables beside my woo-woo books and palo santo sticks. I'd put it all out. All my mala beads and everything. Lee was gone. This was my house. I'd party in it like I wanted and needed to.

I added my favourite spirits to the pared-back bar stock. And that was it. "You want a drink? You're going to have one of my favourite drinks." "You want some food? Here's a meal I can handle—barbeque steaks, some potatoes, and a veg. If you don't like it or I screw it up, we'll order pizza." There was no more keeping up with the Joneses. It was going to kill me if I kept trying. So, I started doing things my way, and guess what? I came to this: If people don't like it, they don't have to be in my life.

Reframe Family Rituals

Day by day and event by event, I found ways to reframe my situation and discover myself and the fun in things I once thought I could only enjoy as someone else's "other half." I muddled my way through the first set of major holidays, especially the Christmas season.

My favourite holiday tradition has always been decorating the Christmas tree, and my kids love it just as much. There was no way around it, so I brought out the box and, like I had on that first transition day, tried to pretend for their sake that everything was fine. One by one, I pulled out the ornaments. Each had special meaning to me. Over the years, I'd collected memories and feelings I thought would be evergreen but were now dry and fragile. I choked back tears as I unwrapped each. I had to keep getting up to go to the bathroom or mud room for bawling sessions.

Then I'd pull myself together and go back into the living room. As the kids played and hung their favourites, I quietly discarded the ones that no longer fit. There was the engagement ornament, new house ornament, bringing home baby, all the milestones of our life together now haunted me like ghosts of Christmases past.

Then, we got to the angel. The angel is the icing on my children's Christmas cake. Daddy always placed the angel on the top of the tree, and now I wanted to burn that fucking angel. Instead, I said as nonchalantly as I could, "I think next year we should come up with a new topper for our tree." Later, we sat around the table and talked about what mattered most to each of us when it came to holiday traditions and made some plans for how we'd replace some old traditions with new ones. Some things you can squash immediately. Other things, like angel tree toppers, need to be phased out.

This works with kids of all ages and just about any size of family. We can usually hit two if not all three of everybody's top priorities with some creative problem solving. It's not always perfect. Sometimes there is a little bit of sadness. But, in the end, the old traditions are remembered, not regretted.

Last Thanksgiving, we were so busy doing fun things that we came up with a list of simplified traditions and rituals. At the end of the day, my kids remarked on how quiet it was and how small our dinner table was because it was just the three of us. But it worked out fine. I still made the turkey

For every family tradition that you've carved out, there's **always a new one that can be made.**

and fixings, and we were together. We focused on what we could do and what was most important. So, for every family tradition that you've carved out, there's always a new one that can be made. And for every together tradition, there's opportunity to carve out a solo one.

Establish Independent Rituals

Our shared custody agreement meant the kids would spend Christmas Eve with their dad. I'd never spent Christmas Eve alone. For the first time in my life, every member of my family was celebrating Christmas Eve without me. It was the most depressing, awful, and ultimately positive experience I'd ever had.

Instead of hiding or numbing out with alcohol or a food binge, I decided to carve out new rituals for myself. I knew it was going to hurt *a lot*, but the upside was that, because I was alone, I was one hundred percent in control. I decided first and foremost how I wanted to feel. Like, did I want this to be social? I'd been invited by friends to several events and could have found other things to do, but I knew I wanted to be alone to sit with everything I was feeling. So, I chose to stay home.

I also knew that I wanted to be comfortable. I got myself a new onesie. (There's the Canadian in me for sure.) I wanted a fire and a glass of wine. I wanted to watch a *Sex and the City* movie. I wanted to have a bath, and I wanted to go for a walk.

I wasn't attached to anything on my list. If it didn't happen, that would be fine as long as I was doing something that had meaning to me and helped me feel the way I wanted to feel. Each thing on my list represented that bigger goal without having any pressure attached to it. But you know what? I did all of them. I also ended up talking on the phone with a girlfriend, who was also newly separated, for about two hours that evening. We just shot the shit and enjoyed our friendship.

The highlight of that night, though, was a fresh, beautiful snowfall. It was one of those warm, snow-falling nights, which are my favourite. I stepped out of my house and into the "Auld Lang Syne" scene in the *Sex and the City* movie. It felt just like that. I breathed in the clean air, absorbed the picture perfectness of the moment, and thought, *You know what? It's okay.*

It wasn't that I wasn't sad, but it was okay to be sad. I wasn't afraid to be in that space. It just was what it was.

13

· · · · ·

Meeting Your Former Partner's New Love Interest

JUST LIKE holidays, we can pretty much guarantee that, at some point, another romantic interest is going to come into our former partner's life and into the family dynamic. Even though it was painful to contemplate, I'd anticipated this and worked through with my therapist some of my feelings and how I'd respond. Because I faced my fears and was connected to my values and my vision for what I wanted in my life and my children's lives, and because I was getting better and better at self-care, I knew what I needed.

I had done the pre-work and asked Lee to give me ample notice before he introduced someone to the kids. Doing that would allow me time to process my emotions about what was happening. He said, "Sure, no problem."

Not long after that conversation, Lee told me he was with someone and wanted to introduce her to the kids within the next few weeks. I said, "Great. Thanks for letting me know." It was all quite blasé on the surface.

You'll Always Be the Motherfucking Mommy

Even if you do have the luxury of a heads-up, that doesn't mean you're just going to accept it on an emotional level. When I got the confirmation, I found myself climbing a mountain and having to stop and unpack that backpack to see what was really chafing me and weighing me down.

My problem was that I believed my children were going to have someone they were going to like better than me, their mom. And someone else was going to be playing family with my family. And someone else was going to experience all the things that I'd worked hard to create for my life.

In short, I was jealous.

Once I could put words to my feelings, I asked for advice from a girlfriend of mine whom I respected and trusted and who'd been through a divorce herself. Before I could put the period on the end of my sentence, she said, "Oh, no, no, no, no. You are the motherfucking mom. Like, that's it. Nobody, *nobody* will ever take that away from you."

She reminded me to think about the other woman. "Think about *her* job. She's not Mom. She actually has to live in your shadow. Right? *And* she's taking care of your ex, so he's happier. Therefore, your children are happier. And you know what it was like to manage him, so hallelujah. You should be thanking God for her."

That was all it took. I wasn't losing my children at all, and this other person was probably even more nervous about this first in her new relationship than I was about this first in my divorce journey. With that in mind, I considered how to make our first introduction or first drop off with the kids less awkward. My therapist suggested that I write her a letter or invite her to meet me for coffee.

I thought about that and decided I wasn't up for a coffee date, but I did like the letter idea.

Be Gracious

My letter was an email (because this isn't 1954), but it had all the customary niceties. I acknowledged that this was new territory for all of us and welcomed her to our family. I conveyed my heart: that putting the children first was most important to me, which included figuring out how to operate as a blended family.

Feel free to use my words as a template for your first encounter:

> Hey, [Name].
>
> I write to you today to break the ice—a small token of my sincere appreciation for your relationship with Lee and the special person you are and will continue to become with the children.
>
> As you know, Lee and I are committed to being the best co-parents we can and this certainly includes you and all the many qualities that you share with us.
>
> The kids speak fondly of you and the fun that you have together. As you can imagine, it is a process for me to accept another person joining their lives and it also warms my heart to know how good you are to them. I know it is the very beginning and we will have much time to figure out how all this messy stuff works out, but I want you to know that I absolutely embrace you as an important part of my children's lives and therefore an important part of our family.

I do look forward to finally seeing you and my hope is that it will be a little less awkward with some dialogue beforehand. I do wish the best for you and Lee and all the many blessings this new blended family has—most importantly our health and happiness!

With loving kindness and respect,

Alicia

Her response was swift and warm. She told me that she couldn't imagine what I was going through and was thrilled that I'd reached out to her the way I did. She went on to say that she was committed to being a team player by supporting whatever decisions Lee and I made regarding our children. She was willing to partner to support our family goals.

With that, all potential bombs were defused; by the time we met each other face to face, we had already established a rapport. It wasn't awkward for the kids, and I felt great about it.

Here's the funny part. Sometimes there's this tongue-in-cheek thing like, "Oh yeah, wow. That was really kind and gracious of you," but the implication is that it was a strategic move on my part. Like, "Hey, sister. I'm the motherfucking mom. And *I* welcome *you* to *my* family." I can honestly say that it wasn't like at the time. I hadn't thought about it that way. I was only trying to anticipate my needs and understand my insecurities, and I wanted to script a better scenario for myself than the one I could see playing out if I stewed in my own juices and did nothing.

I can imagine that this is activating for some of you reading this, especially if your former spouse left you for another person or if they came out to you in a way that upset your understanding of their gender identity or sexual orientation. You might be swirling in a sea of profound confusion,

How we respond internally and externally, **in private and in public, matters.**

overwhelming grief, and raw anger, and this may sound like one more unicorns-and-rainbows message that only works under lab conditions. That's fair. Hell hath no fury and all that because, yeah, that's your reality.

Here's what I've learned from working with women like you. (And this overlaps with the journey we're walking together.) First, acknowledge that you feel betrayed and that the way you might want to react to that is by taking control of whatever you can, and kids and custody are a way you can do that. It can be a way to hit 'em where it hurts and keep hitting as often as opportunities present themselves. Second, understand that if you choose this path now, you choose this for your future.

How we respond internally and externally, in private and in public, matters. This is a big deal.

It's natural for us to not want them to have this. It's natural for us to want to turn the screws. But I can almost guarantee that you'll meet someone who is a big enough part of your life that you'll want to introduce them to your kids. If you want to go on a special date or a trip together, you may need to ask your former partner to rearrange the agreed-upon custody schedule. Whatever the case may be, your former partner and your new love interest are likely going to interact in some way. This is your opportunity to set the tone and demonstrate how you expect to be treated when your turn comes.

Model Greatness

It can be a significant emotional challenge to always take the high road. I know from experience. Lee and I did not always act amicably. My healing and our healthy, co-parenting relationship was five years in the making. At that stage of the game, we were barely talking and pretty much hated each other. But that's the point: A lot of this has to do with how we choose to behave despite the circumstances. Remember, I'm not talking about faking it until you make it. I'm talking about making a conscious choice to act out your highest values even when you don't feel like it. Everything we have walked through together between chapter 1 and this point has been about helping you find peace and happiness and to be a person your children and others look to for stability and leadership.

Writing that email and doing the friendly kid-swap meeting were empowering. It moved me closer to how I want to feel on an ongoing basis.

If you're facing this big first, I hope that you feel that this is *your* moment. You chose to model greatness before you got to this moment. This is an opportunity for you to truly step into your power and exercise moral authority.

The more we extend the olive branch and use long-term thinking, the more we foster a new type of experience and engagement. When we earn moral authority, we can rest in the knowledge that things are likely to go better for us in the future. And even if they don't (because we have no control over other people), we'll have the skills to self-soothe and the confidence to keep on going and growing.

And the thing is, you don't want that other person back anyway. You might think you want to go back to them for all the fantasy reasons, but you don't. You may be wanting to argue with me here. That's fine, but at some point you'll understand what I'm saying. You no more want that marriage back than your former partner does. It's over. You're moving forward in a healthier, more authentic way. The two of you came together and have a legacy to be proud of and to respect. And that's it. Moving forward and not being attached to your children's other parent in any romantic sense doesn't diminish the relationship you had. It's part of your past and not

We need to stay grounded and be supportive and enthusiastic about their news. **This is their life.**

much more than wallpaper in the present. If we stay emotionally stuck in the past and let our negative emotions guide our actions, we run the risk of putting our kids in very uncomfortable situations.

One of the best ways for us to model greatness is to pull our kids into the conversation and establish behaviour expectations. We might prepare our children to meet this new person by saying something like, "Hey, listen. This is how I expect you to treat this other person because this person is important to your father." This goes back to those elevator speeches I recommended having ready to recite in chapter 6. If we take it even further, we can have a discussion with our kids about their own values and how their instincts and actions are lining up with their highest values in this situation. We don't always need to dictate behaviour. Kids are smart and kind and often come up with their own creative and endearing solutions to problems we adults struggle to work through.

But we must avoid the temptation to fish for information or use our kids as messengers. Have you ever experienced those little cheap digs after your child has come back from time with their other parent, or with someone else who doesn't have the warmest feelings for you? Something a child innocently brings up but you know the person who said it was hoping it would get back around to you? It sucks, and it's unproductive.

On the flip side, sometimes our children are going to come back with information and feelings about others. They might not like their other parent's new romantic interest. That can leave us in a tight spot. We don't want to have a gossipy mindset, thinking, *Ooooh. Trouble in paradise?* We really want to treat others the way we want to be treated. That means we can't poison the well. But we also need to honour

our children's need to process their emotions. We can listen objectively and offer values-oriented advice because it's not our place to judge, and we know by now that there are at least three sides to every story. We lean in with curiosity to our child's thoughts and feelings, discuss their value systems, and focus on the choices they want to make. What's important is that we're giving our child the skills to go back to their other parent and deal with it, just like we would if they had to deal with a teacher or a coach or a friend.

As I've said before, I'm not talking about learning that our child is being neglected or abused. Our child's physical safety and mental health always comes first. If there's abuse, report it to the proper authorities. If it's a personality conflict, show your child how to deal with difficult people when you can't simply avoid them.

Then there are those times when our kids just *love* this new person. They come home bubbly and in full-on share mode. They're excited. They're happy. They're having a great time. Each story, each expression of admiration, can be a punch to the throat of our soul. During those times, we need to stay grounded and be supportive and enthusiastic about their news. This is their life.

Letting Go and Gaining More

Modelling greatness takes self-awareness, mental toughness, and above all practice. But it pays off in every area of our lives, and it's a gift we give to our precious children because their other parent is (hopefully) going to be in their lives for a very long time, and that parent is going to bring their own people into the mix.

So I say the more, the merrier. Maybe this new person will be someone who loves to coordinate birthday parties and do all those things I can't do or don't have any interest in doing. At the end of the day, all I want is for my kids' lives to be better. The more people there are to love and support them, the better.

Some people say things like, "Alicia, I frankly have no desire to have this happy, blended family situation. He can do his own thing. I'm going to do my own thing."

That's fine. Everybody has their own values and needs. But my belief is that, whether we like it or not, that new person is now part of the family for however long they stick, and that means they're going to be around for occasions when we can't just do the kid trade-off thing. I'm talking about graduation ceremonies and weddings, events when the focus should one hundred percent be on our child and when—in my mind—we shouldn't bring anything into that space that would diminish the joy of the day. Parents who can't countenance each other or even act like decent human beings in public for the greater good, well, that strikes me as selfish. Besides, holding onto that level of resentment just takes too much damn energy. Maybe I am selfish after all, but I want to keep my vibes high and my batteries fully charged so I can be the best motherfucking mommy I can possibly be and scoop out for myself every last bit of deliciousness this life has to offer.

14

· · · · ·

Single Mommin' It

EVEN THOUGH I'd had plenty of time to contemplate it, I didn't anticipate how hard the reality of being an on-my-own mother would be. I felt alone because I wasn't a proper single mother. That is, I didn't technically qualify. I mean, my kids have a dad. And that dad is very much a part of their lives. This brought up the whole label thing again.

I didn't identify with being a divorced person or an ex-wife. I didn't identify with being "jealous," or a "drama queen," or a "scorned woman," or a "single mom." But what was real to me was that what I was doing was go-it-alone parenting.

Single Parenting versus Co-parenting

Single parenting and co-parenting have their unique challenges. Single moms are completely on their own without the other parent's support. They may have full control, but they have zero recovery time. Co-parents must negotiate or split control and are subject to the other person's drama. These are distinct experiences. Both are difficult, but truly single moms have the hardest job.

I've chosen to embrace all of us as single moms because when our children are with us, we're doing the mom thing all by ourselves. I want to honour that fact for all of us and to discourage the mentality of *Oh yeah, well, you're lucky because x, y, z* that sometimes comes up. Comparing pain and placing others above or below us on a hierarchy of need is counter-productive. My goal is to find common experiences and help you find hope and empowerment, even though I'm offering advice from my perspective as a co-parent rather than as a precisely defined single mom. If you're a single mom, I hope you're able to take things from this chapter that will improve your experience and that you'll forgive me if at any time my privilege blinds me to your needs.

Regardless of our exact situation, what's important is that we carve out as much control as we can and use it to create a healthy environment for ourselves and our kids. We do this by continuing to cultivate our mindset and by taking ownership of our actions, improvising when we need to, and boldly but graciously stating our needs and boundaries. The blessing in all of this is that it provides an opportunity to develop better relationships with our children and to be healthier, happier role models. Children with the benefit of having two parents who share custody also benefit from seeing each parent as distinct, and often learn to value their moms and the time they get to spend with them because they don't have access to them all the time.

Time apart encourages healthy boundaries and forces us to take time for ourselves. When we all gather around the family table again, we can do it with fresh perspective. If we use the time apart from our kids to rest our minds and bodies, we have more energy to be kickass moms. The time apart can help us and our kids develop more balanced, back-and-forth-type relationships.

When we improve our resiliency and get good at self-care and honest communication, we get better at working with our former partner to define shared values and establish mutual goals. How we accomplish those goals may look different depending on which house the kids are in at the time, but we're all working toward the same general thing. The most important thing is to not judge or critique or do any negative things through the children or otherwise, like we talked about in previous chapters. What we're doing is setting up a parenting lifestyle that works specifically for us. It's about finding a family flow that matches our values and shows the way we've decided to live our life. Because, for me, a lot of how I was doing family was not true to how I chose to parent when I settled into single mommin'.

What's Your Forte?

In my previous life as a married parent, my partner valued planning and the structure provided by a rigid schedule. This applied to everything, right down to our meals. We sat down together at scheduled times for every meal, and the table was always set a certain way—napkins out, specific foods on serving platters. Everything was created and served a specific way and the quality needed to be exceptional. For me, each meal came with an appetizer of stress. The pressure of perfection sucked the joy out of sharing time and a meal as a family. The expectation was perfection, which is not achievable. That requirement meant I was failing every time I sat down at the dinner table.

When I started single mommin' it, I realized that my parental forte is to love, connect, and be in the moment, to experience my children's lives with them instead of observing it from a distance or hearing about it later. Trying to force myself into structure, routine, and Emily Post– and partner-approved standards of etiquette was not only a drag but a soul crusher. I let those things go—and not gradually, baby. As soon as it was just me, I started living in the moment in a real and present way.

I often don't have any clue what we're having for dinner until it's dinnertime. My brain doesn't like to be bothered by having to think about that when there are more important things to do and think about during the day. If I haven't figured it out by dinnertime, we order pizza or do something else that's easy. I honour and embrace my mediocre mom chef Self and am delighted that my kids think of me as the best Kraft Dinner maker (yes, with hot dogs and ketchup), a fact that would have embarrassed me in the past. Back then I believed that being a good mom and wife meant elite-level cooking. Now I'm not saying that pizza and mac-n-cheese are staples of my kids' diets. They aren't. But I'm also not saying that they aren't go-tos when life gets busy and there's more benefit to focusing effort on other things.

And so what if we don't eat at 6:30 every night. Maybe we're hungry at 4:00 or maybe 8:30. That's okay. Sometimes we have dessert before dinner because that's when we want it and other times we have it after. Sometimes we don't have it at all. We look at the big picture and say, "What do we feel like doing right now? We've got three hours to work with. How do we want to approach this?" If we decide to grab a snack and go for a hike, fine. We do that. Sometimes we end up grazing the whole night and don't sit down to a formal meal. That's okay too.

We often eat simple healthy dishes that I prepare in advance and plate in the kitchen to save time, dishes, and stress. The magic of carefree cooking means spending more quality time with my kids in and out of the kitchen. It fits

We've got to figure out what **we must do, what we want to do, and what we can do.**

with who I am and what I value. I like to do all my work in the kitchen and quickly wash the pots, pans, and utensils as I go. Then I like to sit down to a relaxed meal and pile the dirty dishes in the sink for cleanup in the morning.

Even though I'm looking to the next day for when I'll wash those dishes, I'm the type of person who doesn't like to wake up and plan out my entire day. I prefer to check in with myself and see how I feel and what I need to do to get myself to feel the way I want to feel. I may decide that I want to do something active in the morning, then have a nap and then maybe do something else that's active or social in the afternoon. I don't want to plan it out exactly, and I certainly don't want to think about what's for dinner while I'm having my morning coffee. Does that mean I never plan anything? No. I'm a grown-up and a business owner. I live in the real world, one that's arranged around a calendar and revolves around a clock. But I don't let those things be the boss of me when they don't need to be.

For me, the balance and opportunity in this is teaching kids about structure, not necessarily regimen, because at the end of the day we are human beings who crave and need some amount of routine. That's especially true when we have little humans depending on us. So as much as I am a free spirit, it would be absolute anarchy living like that all the time. Even on days when I don't feel like doing the mommy thing, I do the best I can and show my kids that they don't have to be perfect. They just have to show up and make themselves proud.

I've also conditioned my kids to let everything go every once in a while. This is almost always on a weekend when we haven't scheduled anything or aren't following any routine at all. We can go into free spirit mode and do just fine. The kids get it. They roll with it. They enjoy it, just like I imagine they enjoy the benefits of their dad's more structured way of doing things. The bottom line is that I'm energized by changing things up and I am very aware of when I need to recharge my energy by staying quiet and still. I let those things guide me. That works for me. My children's father preserves his peace and energy by sticking to a routine. That works for him. Our children get the benefit of experiencing both modes of operation and will be able to find what works for them faster than they might if they were forced to follow only one way of doing things.

But, of course, our children's lives and our schedules get more complicated and demanding as they get older. The fact is that when our children are with us, we're down a parent. We now have twice the workload. Things start to look different through this lens, and we realize we have to make choices. I might be a free spirit who doesn't want to be overly programmed and overly scheduled, but the kids also want to do things. Finding this balance takes awhile as we try new things and discover what works and what doesn't.

Juggling Roles

When I first started my journey as a single parent, I was still trying to keep pace with my previous life. I was doing all the things but felt tired and defeated, as if I was letting everyone down. That manifested in me being a snappy mom. I was still living by other people's (or what I perceived to be other people's) ideas of what a good mom is. Expectations *are* a bitch, and I was letting them turn me into one.

And all the undue pressure activated my vices and my need to take charge of everything I could. Things quickly spiralled out of control. I thought that getting ahead of things would let me meet my own standards of a good mom, an effective mom, a leading lady type of mom.

Beautiful things start to happen **when we collaborate with our kids.**

I stepped back and realized that transition days were important and that the only activity I could handle on those days was the trade-off. So now, on the Wednesdays when I get my kids, I focus on the emotions of that task and on getting my children squared away back at my house. The most important thing on our agenda that day is to reconnect. Thursdays, for us, are activity days. And I've learned that, each season, I can handle only one extracurricular activity with the kids, which typically take one to two days per week. This is a difficult thing for many single parents because it requires hard choices. We can't be everywhere at once and still maintain our sanity. We probably can't let our kids do competitive hockey *and* dance *and* swimming *and* music lessons. This is a time to assess what we can realistically handle.

Instead of getting caught up in the distraction of doing all the things we think our children want and need (making their lunches every morning, keeping all the laundry clean, putting their clothes for the next day out every night), we need to remember what they really need. Our children need our time, and they need to feel connection to their parents, their home, and themselves. Doing this requires us to be intentional and very deliberate in the choices we make. It requires that we honour our highest values and protect our energy, so we can be the best parent to our children as we go it alone.

We've got to figure out what we must do, what we want to do, and what we can do.

Plan for Extracurricular Activities

Now, I love a family meeting and always try to stay connected to the fact that my divorce journey is also my children's journey. As we discussed in chapter 12, involving our kids in decision making that affects them empowers them and strengthens their relationship with us. When we realize something's gotta give, it's prime time to gather our family and do some talking. Whenever I start to sense that I'm going to have to cut back on something that involves my kids, we have a family meeting to establish awareness and priorities and to create a plan.

The beauty of this family plan is that it's quick and easy, and it works at every age and stage. I recommend that you do this for yourself and your kids. Many of my clients have found value in it and repeat it as often as needed, because as children get older they tend to want to do more extracurricular activities. Often those activities cost money and take more time than just the actual hour your kid is in that ballet lesson every week.

First, write down how many hours in the week you and your children have to spend together.

Second, list the things you must do. Make the list comprehensive: personal hygiene (bathing, getting ready in the morning, brushing teeth, etc.), grocery shopping, meal prep, homework, packing backpacks, going to school, cleaning our rooms, going to bed, and so on. Estimate how much time each task will take, and note what day the task must be done if it's date specific.

Now this third step is the fun part for the kids and the potentially stressful part for you. Have everybody make a list of things they want to do: hockey, hanging out with friends, having a sleepover at home, for example. If there's a cost to any of these activities, write it down.

For the fourth step, list anything that could be considered a special project. Regular health check-ups at the doctor and dentist fall into this category, as do haircuts and having the oil changed in your car. These are infrequent but predictable things, things we might think of as mundane. Your list can also include fun things, such as a remodelling project. What they should have in common is that they take time and need to be planned for, timing wise and financially.

My children and I document our lists on two calendars that we keep within easy reach and view. One calendar is for my stuff. The other is for kids' activities. That way we can compare them and see what we need to do on any given week to accomplish our must-dos and accommodate each other's needs and wants.

In chapter 15 we'll go into more detail about budgeting, but this will give you some idea of the time and financial expenditures you need to make to satisfy the musts and the wants.

When I walk clients through this exercise before they do it with their children, many react negatively. They panic. They realize they can't do it all, and they focus on what they believe are their children's expectations. This makes them feel terrible about themselves and their situation. They stop thinking from a place of abundance and start reacting from a place of fear. In that place, they're likely to go home and blurt out to their child, "Sorry, but you can't do hockey this season. We can't afford it." That hardly seems fair to a child who had no buy-in and just got smacked in the brain with this info, even if it's true that you're going to need to cut back.

In these situations (and believe me, I've been there myself), I encourage women to get ahead of things and do this exercise with their kids. This collaboration can open the door to more inclusive and transparent conversations. Hiding the truth from the kids is no good. Sooner or later, the emotional, physical, and financial pressure will rupture the dam, so you might as well lean into the conflict and further develop the communication skills you've been working on since the day your journey to living an authentic, impactful life began. All the things we've been doing so far, you can do with your children. Beautiful things start to happen when we collaborate with our kids. We gain more control of our lives. Our children gain more control of their lives. And we grow with our kids. Talk about modelling greatness and nurturing our children in ways that will help them be wiser and braver adults.

Once everyone has their lists and understands the big picture, obviously some changes are going to need to be made. Now's the time to identify the problems—which I prefer to call challenges, because it's a more positive word that kind of sounds like a game you can win—and ask our kids for creative solutions that they're comfortable with and that would work for everyone.

Maybe you collectively decide that carpooling is a good option, or that hiring a babysitter or nanny will help with some things. What about the extra cost? Maybe there's a friend or family member who's available and happy to help. What other options are there? If your children are younger and have no concept of how much things cost, they may offer solutions that would put more financial strain on you. It's fine to remind them that there's only so much money in the pot, so the goal is to come up with a way to balance time, energy, and money while getting the most everybody can out of this new life.

It's Okay to Slow Down

I was lucky in many ways because my children were young when their father and I uncoupled. I didn't have to undo anything for them, but many of my clients feel the burden of wondering how they could possibly undo their kids' lives and destroy their sense of normalcy. If anything good came out of the COVID-19 pandemic, I think it's that the lockdowns and constraints levelled the playing field in some ways. It highlighted the fact that we get so busy doing all the things. We've gotten tired. So tired. We've been so busy and so tired that we throw our kids into things and throw money around thinking we can buy them "normal," that we can buy back our old lives and our sense of place in them. That's the price of privilege. It robs us of relationships.

Yes, the pandemic was hard and brought pressures of its own, but many of us (kids included) came to realize that a slower pace offers a chance to breathe, and to engage with each other on a deeper level. Just like the pandemic, being a single mom affords us an incredible opportunity because we're forced to parent in a non-privileged way. There's only one of us, and we have to make shitty decisions, but it all works out in the end. In the end, we're okay. And our kids will be okay.

Single mommin' for real ain't easy. We must do our best and forget the rest. We can't keep up with the Joneses—and those Joneses, they are everywhere! We've gotta learn how to articulate that and help our kids learn to prioritize their needs and wants and develop reasonable expectations of us.

15

· · · · ·

Reinvent Your Career and Finances

DURING MY MARRIAGE, I had a plan. I was on a mission. I was a team player. I'd spent years helping my husband build a business, and I regularly interacted with twenty to thirty people a day in that business. When the word *divorce* came into play, so did our prenuptial agreement.

Overnight, I was ejected from my marriage and the business (or so it felt at the time), divorced from my husband and from my livelihood.

Working women with stable careers may not have to tackle this challenge, but with my marriage went my work identity, my means of earning a reliable income, and the people with whom I'd spent the bulk of my time. Except for the social aspect, this is the situation that many stay-at-home moms face. Sure, you can negotiate for alimony, child support, and a portion of the accumulated assets, but it's not that easy. I bet many of you are thinking, *Ha! Assets. Alimony. That'd be nice, but what about [insert your unique circumstances here]?* Money issues are one of the top reasons couples divorce and one of the top things that keep us up at night as we move through the process.

Fears about our financial future are one of the primary barriers to our happiness too. If we're not careful, we can contract a very bad case of our old friend analysis paralysis again. But those money fears are usually not based on any real analysis. They're based on ruminations about *maybes* and *what ifs*. When we face our fears and focus on how we want to feel, we become empowered and energized to step into our role as leading ladies and onto the stages we've designed. This is our time to earn applause and standing ovations. And even if nobody else cares about or notices what we're doing, we'll have the peace that comes with authenticity and the satisfaction of overcoming adversity in our pursuit of happiness.

When I stepped out of the business and started, willingly or not, down the path of independence, I felt isolated and scared as hell. I no longer had the distractions of work and managing other people. I had to deal with this stuff. I had to work on my own shit and manage myself. I didn't see it at the time, but this was a blessing. Many of the women I work with have jobs they love or have no intention of leaving (or may not have considered switching employers or careers—*yet*). They must put time and energy into their healing journey while managing the pressure that comes with the divorce process and the requirement to maintain their reliable employee and leadership roles. When I recognized that blessing and adopted even the slightest bit of an abundance mindset, it reinforced my growing awareness that this whole divorce thing was an opportunity to reinvent myself.

I moved from not having the strength to even get out of bed some days to being able to pick up a pad of paper and a pencil and put a big you-are-here X on my financial map.

From there, I could choose the route that would get me to my desired destination.

The B-word

Now we come to the dreaded *budget.* Figuring out where we are financially can seem easy, or it can feel like an overwhelming task. The reality is that many married women have no real understanding of the family finances, especially if their partner has been the primary breadwinner. While we may do most of the grocery, clothing, and other shopping, we aren't always equal partners in how money gets spent, and we often don't know where it's going and when. If the thought of creating a budget is causing your stomach to twist, relax. It's just math, and only the adding and subtracting part.

In case you're new to this, *budget* simply means the balance of income and expenditures. In plain English, it's how much money is coming in versus how much is going out, the goal being more in than out.

This will be easier or a bit more challenging depending on where you are in the divorce process. If you've already parted ways and all the negotiation is done, you know how much is in the bucket. This is when reality hits for many women because they realize that, as a single parent, they really are working with less. They aren't, therefore, going to be able to maintain the same lifestyle that their kids are used to. That sucks. It's a real-world thing.

So, what if you have a deficit?

Don't panic.

Seriously. First, the divorce process is like moving. It's expensive with all the one-time fees and all the bits and bobs you may need to purchase to replace the things your former partner took with them. Once you get a little past it, your financial position will likely improve even if only by a little. Second, fear is a motivation killer and a creativity killer. It's like slamming on the brakes. Don't risk locking up your wheels and skidding off the road. Keep your eyes open and facing forward and your hands on the wheel while you consider your options.

When I first realized that I didn't have a handle on this part of my life, I thought, *I have to learn about money. I have to learn about financial investments. I really need to get better at this.* The goal was correct, but my emphasis was wrong. I was putting undue pressure on myself and kind of judging myself because I didn't know these things. When I thought more about it, I realized, *Wait. I don't need to be an expert at that. I need to have a team around me that can get me there, whether it's H&R Block, financial self-help books, a personal accountant, or a financial advisor.* The point is that we don't need to know all the things and be all the things. We just need to take responsibility for our financial situation and do what it takes to correct anything that's unclear, and then build for our future.

In chapter 3 we talked about how this thing is too big to do alone. If you have hang-ups about money, like so many of us do, this is a good time to talk to a professional or two. You might need to explore with a licensed therapist why you overspend or stay in a state of fear even when you have enough to live month to month or even to weather unexpected storms. You might want to talk to your investment advisor. You might want to talk to your life coach about setting up some accountability guard rails. Knowing where you are, where you want to go, and the route you want to take to get there doesn't matter if you can't get the car moving or if you keep compulsively changing lanes and directions.

It's hard to overemphasize how important this part is because some of us are in deep trouble at this stage—genuine,

We don't celebrate divorce, but we can see it for the chance it offers **to recreate our personal and professional lives.**

no-fault-of-our-own trouble. I work with women who are living in subsidized housing and working several jobs and absolutely busting their humps to make ends meet. They grind every day, and most days there's no light on the horizon. Other clients come from more privileged backgrounds. Their challenge is the tyranny of Instagram perfection and keeping up with the Joneses. It's easy to get sucked into despair and give into the temptation to use credit cards and other means to keep our kids happy and our appearances up.

That's a hole that's often pleasant to dig ourselves into, but it goes straight to hell. When we find ourselves in a hole, we've got to get out fast. The sooner we can do that, the better off we are. There's the self-respect, authenticity aspect, but there's something else at play that can be hard to appreciate in the moment. In this analogy, I'll call it our runway.

Think about what it takes to lift a plane off the ground and have it take flight. The younger you are, the more runway you have to establish a sustainable career and store what you need for retirement. Time naturally shortens our runways, but overspending and taking on debt also makes our airplane heavier, requiring a longer take-off roll.

If you're on the back end of the divorce process and the ink is dry and signatures set, you have everything you need to figure out exactly what financial constraints you're operating under. If you're in the process of getting a divorce, I recommend walking through this exercise while keeping in mind that there are probably more opportunities open to you. If you can foresee potential financial pitfalls, you might be able to negotiate a settlement that puts you in a better financial position than you'd end up in if you go in misinformed or leave it to chance.

As I said, finding out where you are is a fairly straightforward process. To do this personal audit, make a list of all sources of income and when they come in. Having a calendar handy will help. You might want to use a green pen or coloured pencil to write down the source and amount in the calendar block. Now, gather all your bills: mortgage or rent, utilities, car loans, insurance, credit cards and anything that gets automatically charged to them, and anything else that's a regularly due bill. Next, make a list of other predictable outputs: groceries, gas, clothing, and so on. Somewhere in this will be any extracurricular activities your children want to participate in, as well as any health club or other memberships you might have.

Most people talk about monthly budgets, but you'll notice different things when you look at your financial picture at different levels: yearly, monthly, biweekly, and even weekly. Are you cash positive or negative? If you have all the money you need and no concerns, great. But chances are most of you want to go have an ugly cry. Go ahead. I've been there. I'll wait.

Okay. Now, are you ready to take control and move toward your goals while honouring your needs?

The first thing to consider is the thing that is most people's biggest financial expenditure and the one that's most emotionally loaded. Our homes.

When I talk to women about finances and suggest that they do an audit of their situation, many state outright that moving from their home is off the table. They say they aren't even willing to discuss it. They're emotionally attached, they say, and think their children are too. I believed the same, and it's fine to think that. There's nothing wrong with it. We just need to see if we can afford it now and in the long run, and what potential long-term financial effects it will have on us. To these clients I say, "Let's talk cost benefits: pros, cons. This is a financial play. It's also an emotional play and a resource play. So, where do we value this out?"

If we look strictly at the finances part, there are two questions to ask at the beginning of this process:

1 What does it cost to stay in your home?

2 What's the actual benefit of moving to a less expensive place if you need to?

The cost of running a home with a property is not the same game as the cost of running a condo or an apartment without a property. Make a big financial shift if you need to, but understand what you're gaining and losing in the transaction. My thought is that if a major change, especially one where you're losing equity, only moves the dial five or ten percent, is it worth moving the children out of their community, their school district, and giving up all the other things you love and want out of the home you now live in? If staying in the original family home is important to you, can you make up that shortfall in other ways?

I believe that our decisions should be driven by our awareness of where we're at and where we need to be, and by an understanding of how the middle will get us there. Most of those middle things have far less emotion attached to them, so making decisions about them can be easier.

From this group of things, cut the simple stuff first. Got a monthly subscription that you never think to use? Gone. Doggie grooming when you can easily wash your pooch in the kitchen sink? Gone (the groomer, not the dog). High-priced, all-inclusive gym membership when buying a package for the one class you actually show up for is cheaper? Gone. Home grocery delivery service? Gone. Piano lessons you're forcing on your kids because for some reason you think everybody should play an instrument? Gone, along with why you ever felt pressured into that idea in the first place. These changes can add up, and you may be able to save enough in the first few months or year to pay off a debt or sock away some emergency money.

Next, consider how to save money on the must-haves, and remember to think big picture. Can you get a lower interest rate by switching credit cards, or can you switch your miles to cash rewards? What money could you find by shopping for bulk items at Costco versus the grocery store or for groceries at Walmart versus Metro? The thing to remember here is that you're not going to find bags of money by doing this. These changes offer you incremental gains. We do these things because they add up. They do matter. But we soon see that such small changes aren't going to dramatically turn the dial.

Making dramatic financial shifts is hard to do. Some of us will be forced to downsize and move. We will grieve for the loss and probably go through our share of anger, but if we can think of this as a test of our developing skillsets and as opportunities to learn new things and create new spaces for ourselves—and help our children do the same—we win. In all of this, we're reinventing ourselves, not the wheel. What I mean is that we're seeing the world as it is, working with what we have, and coming up with creative ways to use it to get us where we want to go.

How Much Runway Do You Have?

I want to take a minute to talk to those of you in the negotiation phase. Some of the women I meet with are fighting for every last penny that's rightfully theirs or that they can squeeze out of their former partner. They're often still in the fear or anger phase, so I gently try to help them tease out why they're fighting so hard. They say things like, "I'm just losing so much money in this divorce." "I'm not giving up a

Fear is a motivation killer and a creativity killer. **It's like slamming on the brakes.**

hundred and fifty grand." "No way I'm just going to roll over and walk away!"

I admire the chutzpah, but here's the deal: If you're in your twenties or thirties or even early forties, you might have enough runway to make up for those losses. We've got to step back and think about the big picture. If you're going to pay an attorney seventy-five Gs to get you one fifty, you're only up seventy-five. Does that make sense in the big scheme of things? And how much is your time, energy, and peace worth? Sometimes it's best to look ourselves in the mirror and say, "Pull yourself up by your bootstraps, Sally. It's time to get on with it!"

We can't afford to let our ego take over when so much is at stake. If the cost benefit analysis says, *Let this money go and go grab it elsewhere*, what's really up with our "personal stand" or "boundary lines"? This illustrates why it's so important to identify our true values and commit to living up to them even when it sucks, even when to outsiders we look foolish, even when to rage and rule would be oh so satisfying in the moment.

We must get our minds right so our feet can move on.

There are a lot of variables here, though. If you're fighting because you don't have a lot of runway and that seventy-five thousand or whatever dollars will make a significant difference for you, negotiate with the help of a professional the best deal you can for yourself by all means.

These stresses and audits aren't necessary for my clients who got fair settlements and are firmly planted in their careers. They can stay marching forward for the foreseeable future. But the bottom line for myself and for most of my clients is that, regardless of our divorce settlements, we need more money coming into the household. So, we need to work. For stay-at-home moms, it can be scary and hard to know where to start.

Translatable Skills and Career Assessments

For some women, their job is the only stable thing in their life, and one of the few things that brings a sense of control during the divorce process. For most others, this is a time to either enter or reenter the workforce or to make a radical change.

Women entering or reentering the workforce often feel a sense of inadequacy because they aren't familiar with the latest technologies, organizational structures, or varying work cultures. It's a lot to take in. We might not believe that what we've been doing as moms and "homemakers" is tied to the outside world, so we may feel like we have little control. The reality is that we have more control than we think because many of the skills we've been practicing as kid wranglers, grocery shoppers, and PTA moms are practical and transferable.

If you've been a stay-at-home mom and are down on yourself for that, let me encourage you. When I was working in organizational development, I was responsible for hiring team members. I've gotta tell you: I loved hiring women who were coming off maternity leave, and watching the changes in women who were coming back after a long break in employment due to childrearing. Those are some kickass women. They can deal under pressure, they're quick to improvise acceptable solutions to urgent problems, and they manage their time well because they've got to.

I mean, nothing teaches grace under pressure more than milk leaking out of your boobs and soaking your shirt at every squeak from a kid or animal. And nothing teaches you to keep your cool than holding a tiny, fragile, wailing newborn at 1:04, 2:51, 3:37, and 5:02 a.m. And nothing teaches you who to coddle and who to tell to pull themselves together like managing a colicky six-week-old, a rambunctious four-year-old, and a pot-stirring fifth grader. Right?

Stop thinking and playing small. The next time you feel small, remember who you are. If you're still sane and wearing shoes that match, you're actually overqualified for this job called life. And if you figured out how to get through that stage and reach today in spite of everything you've been hit with over the past few months or years, you can figure out this job thing.

Still not sure? Think back to the times you've been in charge of a household project. If you're reading this book, chances are your former partner was out making money while you managed home stuff. Or you were working too but were still the point person for big projects. Maybe you were in charge of a renovation. You led by sourcing materials or contractors. You put together the budget and managed the people to stay within it. When the budget got blown, you were there to determine why and to make decisions about how to handle unforeseen changes. You managed the timeline, paid the invoices, and signed off on the final work. That's job stuff. In fact, that's management-level job stuff.

Whether your experience is with meal planning, vacation planning, extracurricular activity scheduling and transportation management, home renovation, lawn care, whatever... you have experience and translatable skills. Some of us have soft skills; some have more hard skills. You just need to find the job that fits those skills and lets you use the ones you most enjoy exercising.

When I was working in recruitment, we started using an employee reliability index test on applicants. It was interesting, especially when Lee and I took the test and failed miserably. According to the assessment, we'd make astoundingly unreliable employees because we're both (in spite of the co-dependence I suffered from back then) independent people. We like to be in control.

That was good information to have when I started considering my income-producing options and asking myself if I should go back to school, or get a clock-in, clock-out job, or start my own business. There are all kinds of great strength and job assessment tools available. Whether you're entering or reentering the workforce or thinking this might be a good time to change career paths, I recommend taking a few to see where they overlap and what direction they may be pointing you.

At every stage of this journey, I find myself pausing to appreciate that with each step forward, we're getting closer to living a life that nurtures our minds and spirits and reflects our authentic selves. So it was a divorce that shoved us down this road. When we start to heal, we see that divorce was the pattern disruption that opened up new doors. Years after that first horrible day on this journey, I still shake my head in wonder at the profound appreciation I have for the opportunities divorce brings. We don't celebrate divorce, but we can see it for the chance it offers to recreate our personal and professional lives.

Education, Entrepreneurship, and Employment

I think it's important to remember that each of us has our way of travelling. Some of us are interstate, get-there-as-fast-as-possible kinda gals. Some of us are drive-slowly-and-look-at-the-scenery, back-road kinda people. Some of us want to drive ourselves. We might be thought of as business owner gals. Others like to carpool, or see the value in public transportation. We might think of those options as being great fits for small, locally owned businesses or corporate or government work. Each road and speed has its own pros and cons. We don't judge the path; we just need to pick the one that's best for us.

And most of us can change our minds after we've turned down a road. There are rest stops and byways and alternate routes we didn't even know existed. And, of course, there are going to be "do not enter" signs, detours, and accidents along the way. The only thing we need to know right now is where the hell we are, where in this wide-open world we want to go, and what vehicle and how much fuel we have to start our journey with.

There are so many variables to this discussion that one chapter in one book can't address all of them or even come close to painting a picture that shows all the options. But there are three distinct groups of people that I have come across in my work.

First, there are the twenty- and thirty-somethings who typically have enough runway left to take some risks. They may decide to pursue a college or advanced degree, or to start a business. For them, racking up student loans or losing tens of thousands of dollars isn't scary. They can recover, and they want to dive into a particular area of study or business.

Then there are the women of any age who, for whatever reason, need or want (value) a stable job that provides a stable, if not always great, income. They aren't interested in discussing anything that might take them backward financially.

Last, there are the women who've been in stable jobs forever and may be working toward a nice retirement who look up one day and say to themselves, *Oh my God, am I going to do this for the next ten, fifteen, or twenty years?* They often realize that they've fallen into what might be described as the zombie-like stupor of white picket fence syndrome, and now that they've been knocked into a new reality they think, *I am so bored. I just… can't.* They might be scared to death to make a change, or be in a place where the change they want to make isn't wise. What then?

The answer to that question for this last group of women is this: It's simple (but not easy). Make a change or bloom where you're planted. Sometimes we must choose the lesser of two evils. And sometimes we blame our jobs for our dissatisfaction in life. How many times have you heard or said to yourself, "I'm so busy that I can't do such-and-such." But if we look at the situation objectively, the reality is that we weren't prioritizing those things in our lives in the first place. So where does the blame rest: with our work situation or with our own thought and behaviour patterns?

We can stay where we are and, with gratitude, let our work be our means of income and not expect that our job can meet all our needs. We can identify what's missing in our lives and go find it. This goes back to what we started learning in chapter 2. We can explore our options. Find a new hobby or volunteer.

The entire point of all this is to thrive.

What do you need to do to stay emotionally, physically, and financially healthy? There are no wrong answers if we're living an authentic life. We're all needed. We're not all going to be Oprah Winfrey, and we don't need to be. So this is the time to make lists and go back to our old performance reviews and personality tests for guidance regarding what's going to help us maximize our work and the financial aspects of our lives.

When I went through this phase, I told myself, *These are the skills you need. This is the plan to do it. And the reward is thriving through divorce and transforming your life.* I found the sweet spot, the area where my financial needs, my skills, and my passion overlapped, and now I encourage other women to do the same. I can honestly say that I finally feel like I'm living my best life.

The next time you feel small, remember who you are. If you're still sane and wearing shoes that match, you're **actually overqualified for this job called life.**

Forget the Bottom Ten Percent

As I've taken various career assessments and personality tests, I've gained an invaluable kind of outsider's perspective. Knowledge is power. I've always been one for self-improvement, so I've used that knowledge to see where the gaps were and to move forward in better ways. As I've gained confidence by finding my authentic self and modelling greatness, I've shed fear and insecurity. That newfound confidence, coupled with self-knowledge, has led me to a different way of looking at and setting expectations for myself.

I figured that I'd spent a lifetime trying to improve my bottom ten percent and had met limited success. So, I decided to focus instead on my top ten percent, because the results I can get when I focus on applying the full force of my best self are far and away better than the minimal gains I get when I try to improve my bottom weaknesses. I've found that when I focus on my best, I'm happier, healthier, and more productive and efficient.

So many of us lack confidence, lack self-worth, lack self-acceptance, and we get into a victim/martyr space. The truth is we haven't taken responsibility for ourselves and acted as the leaders of our life. We've been supporting actresses, doing all the "right things" for all the "right people." We see personality weaknesses as flaws, something to be fixed before we can step into our power. To make matters worse, we might be doing things we're good at, things that need to be done, but we're not doing things that truly demonstrate our talent and play to our strengths and passion.

"Oh, but that's not *balanced*," we hear. Balance is good, but I think something is missing in that discussion. If you were truly balanced, you'd be operating at fifty percent in every area of your life. Is that what you want? Does that sound like living your best life? I'd rather be chef-ing at ten percent but listening at ninety percent. That's radically unbalanced, but I'd argue that it's more effective for what I—Alicia—want to do in this world. And that is to give one hundred percent of my best self to the things I choose to do.

What would happen if we actually embraced our talents and passions? Imagine how inspired and empowered we'd all be. And just think of the shifts we could make in our lives, our children's lives, and the world if we rose up, kicked those negative voices to the curb, put on our crowns, and said, "Listen up. I rule this place, and I'm about to make shit happen."

The Road Is Challenging, but You Can Walk It

When we harness the power of our potential by efforting, we earn control. It's hard some days, but we just have to take hold of ourselves and decide that we're going to step into the future we want. That means making hard choices, choices that require us to give up one thing to get another, but it's worth it. And we *can* do it.

Don't get me wrong. Some of us are more privileged than others. We need to acknowledge that and back away from toxic positivity and platitudes, but no matter where we are on the spectrum of privilege, we do have opportunities to evolve.

The first part of this book was about taking control of our minds, emotions, bodies, and words. This is an extension of that. We're taking control of our finances. Once we've taken control of all these things, we're truly in control of our lives. That's not to say that bad things won't happen in one area or another, but it's much easier to get control back in one area of our life using the areas we do have control over than to constantly be out of control. The beauty of this stage of our journey is that we've found homeostasis and now have the maturity and skills to add new people and experiences into our lives without the risk of blowing the whole thing up again.

16

. . . . .

Dating and Relationships

NO DIVORCE recovery—or recovery book—would be complete without a discussion about sex and relationships, but finding the right place for this took a lot of thought. Mention it too soon and readers may skim the personal development work to get right to the instant gratification parts of life. But (and maybe worse) mention it last and I risk undermining my own message by implying that this post-divorce journey is about finding and being ready for Mr. or Ms. Forever, that in some way partnering with another person is the last step on our journey or the last piece of the puzzle to make us whole.

Nothing could be further from the truth. I was celibate for two years through my separation because I wasn't ready to be in a romantic partnership. It wasn't that I didn't long to be touched and held and loved and sometimes just flat-out *banged*. It was because I chose to work on myself. I'm convinced that was the most selfless act I could make. I learned so much about myself and about human psychology during that time, which, I'll be honest, is a blessing and a curse.

Today I get frustrated when people put themselves out into the dating world when they're not ready. When we do that, we're messing with another human being's emotions and even their future. I felt a sense of responsibility to myself, to my children, to my family, and to whomever my future partner would be (if a future partnership came to be).

When we're healthy and financially stable, we're in an excellent position to find and attract healthy people like us. The healthier we get, the more our romantic partnerships and friendships become reciprocal: You are giving as much as you are receiving. Who doesn't want that?

Having said that, I do see many people who recouple quickly to share the parental and financial load. If I see true partnership and companionship, I can wholeheartedly support that. But many people recouple because it's comfortable, familiar. They know how to act as a mother or a wife or a whatever label they've adopted and expectations they've taken on. It absolutely can be comforting to know your role, play a familiar part, and stay in a pre-determined space in a relationship. That kind of comfort is often temporary, however.

Here's the thing: Different people have different values and needs. The whole point of this book is to connect with *your* authentic self and decide what you want your life to look and feel like. If that means recoupling sexually, romantically, financially, or whatever sooner rather than later, you do you.

This journey is about exploration and ownership. Whatever we choose, we own it.

Whether you're ready for a partner or not, we're all sexual creatures and ya don't need a warm body to get heated up. This chapter is about finding ways to express your sexual self and satisfy those body cravings with or without another body. 'Cuz, girl, this is part of the experience!

But have you ever thought something like, *Yay. Hoorah. Girl power. I own this. I'm ready to have some fun and start thinking about putting myself out there*... and then looked down and thought, *What the actual hell has happened to my body? I do not own* this *mess. Who switched my bones and bod, and what can I do to get them back?*

Waxing and WonderBras, Wanks and One-Night Stands

Okay, mama. Let's have a girl chat. The kissing, the touching, the sex with a new partner. The thought alone is delicious, but unless you're a tight twenty-year-old, the idea of being naked in front of another human might make your thighs jiggle in fear. And if you've had kids, well, that's a whole 'nother level of *seriously?!*

Break-ups often highlight our insecurities and many of us start focusing more on our physical appearance. Unfortunately, it's often not for healthy reasons. We're often not even focusing on health; we're focusing on conforming to some ideal, what others consider attractive. It becomes less about health and more about "looking healthy." And by looking healthy, of course, we mean looking fit and fabulous. We're trying to prove to ourselves that we've still got it—that we can still get attention from those we desire.

But that's not the point. We aren't trying to attract in the lure kind of way. We're trying to live an authentic life, which automatically attracts the people who are right for us and repels the ones who aren't. Hard-body sex kittens attract a lot of attention, but who's attracted and how does that usually play out over the long run? But, oh, to look like a hard-body sex kitten.

It ain't the glamour life. It's better. It's endearing, boring, beautiful, and **oh so freeing as long as we get there in the healthiest way possible.**

I went to that place immediately. My first thought was *Oh my God, I'm forty and I have to be on the dating scene. If I want to be marketable or attractive to men out there, I need to...*

I did all the things: laser hair removal, Botox, workout routines, wardrobe overhaul, all that stuff, and I wasn't even dating! Despite my choice not to date and my understanding that I needed to work on myself, part of me was still focused on the superficial and what I needed to do to change myself to be acceptable to others, especially men.

My brain was spinning. While I attended to my real health needs, like regular medical exams and girl health stuff, I was thinking, *Oh, right. Now I'm susceptible to cervical cancer. Okay, fine. Do I want an IUD?* Add that to the list of things to talk to my gynecologist about. Then the two-time mommy part of my brain jumped in with *Holy shit, I think my vagina needs to be tighter. I hear bleached assholes are a thing. And like, Brazilian waxing. Landing strip or no landing strip? And what about my boobs? Every time I unhook my bra, those things flop out and unroll themselves. Boob job. I might need a boob job.*

Facial peels. Did 'em. Laser hair removal. Yup. And yes, as I mentioned earlier, I did a coochy tightening thing too. My insecurities and vague sense of what I needed were pulling and pushing me all over the place. You might be feeling that too. It's okay. It's part of our exploration.

I will say for myself that I did two authenticity and healing-oriented things during that time: redoing my wardrobe and focusing on my health (true mental and physical fitness, not reshaping my body). Buying new clothes and getting rid of those I'd worn before felt like shedding my old skin and stepping into a new one, and being more active and making choices that made me feel the way I wanted to feel was transformative. My internal Self changed and those changes manifested outwardly in the way I looked and moved. But I still wasn't ready to wade into the play pool.

A wise person told me early on in my separation that one of the biggest voids would be the lack of physical touch. We need touch, and we need to find ways to be touched. This wasn't a complete shock to my system, and it likely isn't for many of you either. For the two years before we divorced, my former partner and I hadn't had a hot and heavy sex life. But how often had I taken a hug or a passing smile and gentle touch for granted? Those little things were gone when we separated, and I knew they might be gone from my life for good.

I was alone, the most alone I'd ever been. It would have been unhealthy and unfair to expect my children to constantly hug and be near me, so I had to find other nonsexual ways of feeling the warmth and energy of other people. For me that meant regular massages, reflexology, energy work, and acupuncture. I was already committed to trying new things that helped me connect to my authentic self and feel the way I wanted and needed to feel to heal and grow.

But you know what's missing from that picture: toe-curling pleasure.

When the intensity of our intimate encounters started to wane, I convinced myself that I had a low libido and so did my husband. I mean, that made sense, right? We were getting older. We were tired from building a business and raising a family. It all made sense. Right?

As I leaned into my journey of self-discovery, I questioned everything I thought I'd known about myself. I was thoughtful in my exploration and checked in with myself: Do I have a low libido? Because, actually, I feel quite sexual, and very, very horny. Regardless of what I'd tried to tell myself, I was actually coming to the prime of my life, and I was horny as hell while not having as much sex as I really wanted. All right, so I had that self-awareness. Now what?

I boiled everything down to the basics. This journey I had chosen and each step I took along the way was about building a relationship with myself so I can be my best Self and live my best life in every moment with or without someone else on my arm or in my bed. The best answer for me at that time in my life was self-love. It was the icing on my self-discovery cake.

Steamy erotica in the form of books and audible porn, online visual porn, sex toys, and straight-up fantasy scratched that itch for two years. Turns out, I am a very sexual person. Low libido was not the problem.

For some of us, self-pleasure only goes so far. For those people who want someone else to sweat the sheets up with but don't want that person sleeping beside them every night, there's always the one-night stand or the friends-with-benefits arrangement. I'll be honest though. I'm not even sure how a one-night stand works. I'm sure they're awesome in some ways because they're all about lust and passion and excitement and you can be selfish and not have to worry about hurting someone. At the same time, you might be missing a more intimate connection.

Somehow, I knew that what I need is an energetic emotional connection to feel lust and passion. I also need to feel a level of safety before I can let my freak flag fly. One-night stands would make me feel vulnerable and not in the good way. Inhibited. And my journey has been driven by a desire to be connected to others in meaningful ways and to live an uninhibited life.

A friend of mine who was going through a divorce went through a one-night stand phase, and it was great for her. At first it made me wish I could be less rigid about this for myself, but then I stepped back and thought, *No. My needs and wants are my needs and wants. She's a consenting adult and her partners are consenting adults, so there's no moral issue. But it's just not right for me.* And I'm okay with that. It doesn't make me a prude or a scaredy cat any more than it makes my friend slutty or fearless. Those are labels. Other people's labels. This is my body and my life. Until I was ready for another person to be in my life in that way, I wasn't going to let someone be in my body that way. Ya know what I'm sayin'?

I'm now clear about what I need and want out of a partnership. I want a meaningful connection and sex. And when I say sex, I mean *sex*. Delirious sex. And I can't get that from just anyone. Correction. I can't get that *with* just anyone. I can outsource to get a lot of what I need in my life, but I can't just choose the lowest bidder or the person within easy reach. Romance and sex are tied for me. I need both to be healthy and thriving, and I will never compromise or give up on that again.

What about you? What does your ideal sex life look like, and how will you satisfy your emotional and physical needs?

Stay Focused and Step Away from the Beer Goggles

When we do think it's time to add someone into our lives in a romantic sense, that's a good moment to sit down and have an honest conversation with ourselves. I recommend taking out a piece of paper, folding it into quarters, and labelling the four quadrants: "my core values," "my partner qualities," "my relationship top 3 needs," and "my give and receive."

Listing these things out gives us a blueprint before we hit the dating scene. Remove lust, crazy sex drive, and whirlwind fantasies. Stick to facts; actions speak louder than words and anyone who is not in alignment is just No. This blueprint will help you identify what you're most attracted to about a person. Maybe it's spiritual or romantic. Maybe it's intellectual. Maybe it's physical. Whatever it is, write it down and think about it, because you're about to make some significant decisions about what you do with your body, your emotions, and your finances. If those decisions are made from a place of insecurity or are an incomplete picture of who you are and what you need and want, things are not going to end well.

There's a tendency to fall back into the same types of relationships again and again and again. If we don't know who we are and haven't developed the mental and emotional fortitude to hold ourselves within our standards and hold others who don't align with them out, we're going to find ourselves in the same terrible place over and over. Clients sometimes come to me after dating someone for a while, saying, "I'm with a narcissistic partner who's a complete asshole." It's not fun at all, but I approach that head-on by saying, "That's fine. They're probably going to be that way for the rest of their life. The real issue is, Why the hell are you attracted to that?"

If we haven't done our growing up and don't have a clear vision for our future, our attractions can lead us astray. If we know our values and needs, we can see if this person is a good choice for us or if they're just a familiar form because that's all we've ever known. Now that I'm on the other side of divorce and on the mature end of the growth arc as compared to where I was when I started this journey, I'm better able to reflect and state my needs and wants.

I need an independent person who's confident and positive and absolutely capable of taking care of themselves. And they must want to be with me. How they show up every day shows me who they are. When I speak my truth and communicate who I am and what I need, does this person see me and hear me and honour that? Does he choose to be with me and support me as I learn and grow, even if it means I might grow away from him? That's a big deal for me. In the past, I was a co-dependent people pleaser, and I don't want to be that person anymore. I don't want to put on a mask and act out other people's values. And I don't want to be in a committed relationship with anyone who would put on a mask just to be with me.

It's taken a lot of practice to consistently say who I am and what I want without feeling judged for it or feeling like I was risking losing the other person and the connection with them that I valued. When I realized that I was learning from every person that came into my life, it dawned on me that feeling a connection to a person doesn't mean we need to have an intense romantic relationship, or that this person is Mr. Forever. Life was really just giving me opportunities to build a network of friends and acquaintances who each in their own way make my world better. Learning that was extremely freeing. It allowed me to play the long game.

I remember my therapist at some point saying to me, "You know, it's really important to see someone over the course of the year, so you see them through all seasons."

There's so much wisdom in that. Those happy, horny chemicals are most intense in the first few months and maintain their intensity for a max of eighteen months. And what the fairy tales say in terms of love at first sight is all fine and dandy, but we don't live in a fairy tale. We live in the real world, and the real story is that lust blinds us to a lot of stuff. If we want to make smart choices, we've got to flip into our logic brains. The consequence for not doing that is another bad break-up and the heartache it brings. Let's face it: Love is not enough to enter into a relationship, just like falling out of love is not enough to leave it. That may have been why I didn't get physical with the man on the airplane going to the

Feeling a connection to a person doesn't mean we need to have an intense romantic relationship, **or that this person is Mr. Forever.**

meditation retreat, even though I felt a spiritual connection. I think that, deep down, my Self knew what it needed and wanted and refused to put its body into a situation that would in any way hinder progress.

Over time, my mantra has become "I didn't come this far to only come this far."

This came into sharp focus for me when I did start dating. I was with someone for a year and a half. It was an incredible, beautiful, positive experience, but even though he was wonderful in many ways, we couldn't square away our values and goals. Thankfully, I'd come far enough in my journey to see and tell myself plainly that I'd been through the worst break-up I could possibly imagine. I'd been brought to my knees, and I didn't rise through all of that and do all the work that I'd done just to settle again and fall back into old patterns and behaviours. With all that in mind and with no ill will, I decided to "adult" so that we could plan to end our romantic relationship.

Are we going to make mistakes? Yes, of course we are: We're trying new things, testing ourselves, finding our boundaries. But shame on us if we repeatedly fuck things up over wanting to get fucked repeatedly, right?

The good news is that when we know our values and needs and connect with our motivations in any given moment, especially when faced with potentially life-altering decisions, we can make great choices for ourselves and for our kids. And that brings us to those practical considerations.

One of the reasons women jump into another relationship soon after a divorce is because they feel the financial squeeze that being single can bring. It's a fact that it's cheaper for two people to co-habitate and pool expenses than it is for two people to live on their own. Many people partner because a partnership is not just a romantic arrangement, it's a financial arrangement as well. This is one of the reasons I emphasize getting your financial house in order as quickly as you can. Financial independence buys you freedom of choice.

If your motivation for getting into or staying in a relationship is based on financial factors (help with paying the bills, getting free childcare), I'm not here to judge you. Only you know what's best for you. But if that's the only or primary reason you're interested in coupling with someone, then revisit chapter 15 to see what you can do to better position yourself.

I'm grateful to have a different situation. Women like me who are financially independent need to be mindful of the motivations of the other person. Love and lust and all those things may feel good, but I've planned out my financial future for myself. Does that mean that a prerequisite of dating me is to be financially independent? Yes. Does it mean that what's mine is yours and yours is mine? Not necessarily. That's a subject and decision that needs some teasing out. My point is that financially independent women need to watch out for men who love us for our financial assets, not our Self-related assets.

There's another side to consider too, and let's just call it as it usually is. Financially independent working men often couple up fast because they mostly want someone to take care of them and to serve as a nanny to their kids. We can test this by seeing how the other person reacts to not being our number one priority. Hell, if we have kids and a career or calling we love and maybe parents we're taking care of, that person is lucky if they are priority number three or four.

If someone you are dating isn't comfortable with not being the centre of your world, that's a clue that your motivations may be misaligned. It can also indicate that there will be significant practical impacts on your life. We're going to have to find ways to accommodate their needs. And even if their motivations are pure and their needs legit, relationships are a two-way street, give and take. What are we willing to give? If the practical costs of time, energy, or financial resources are too high, then we need to be willing to let that person go. That's the kindest thing we can do: Let them go find someone who fits them and will love them with everything they have. It's also the kindest thing we can do for ourselves because it frees us to find—or not find—the same. Either way, we'll win because we've kept ourselves and our kids as the centre of our world. After all, a healthy relationship requires two independent individuals to bring one hundred percent their best self in a give-and-take that focuses on contribution in all aspects of the relationship.

Timing the Introduction

My children are still quite young and seem fascinated by relationship nomenclature. They often ask me to explain the difference between dating and having a boyfriend. I explain it to them in ways that makes sense to me and see their curiosity as an opportunity—an invitation—to model healthy connections and romance.

Long before I introduced them to any of my romantic interests, they'd met their dad's girlfriend and experienced their dad and his girlfriend's version of romance and what it was like to share a parent and occasionally their home with another adult who was also interested in the loving attention of their parent. When I first thought the time was coming for me to introduce one of my romantic interests to my kids, I struggled with how and when to do it.

I wanted to do it as responsibly as possible, so I talked to my therapist. My therapist didn't mince words. She said, "You can't introduce anyone to your children unless you are certain that this person is going to be around for a long time."

Basically, she was talking about a Mr. Forever. I thought, *Okay, yeah. That makes sense. I don't want to hurt my kids. I don't want them to think I'm slutty or sleazy. And I don't want different men in and out of their home.*

At the same time, there were all these variables, and I felt a great deal of pressure. As I sat there, I went back to what I wrote about in part II of this book and checked in with myself. Was I weighing my options according to my values, or was I letting somebody else's values and labels unduly influence me? The answer was that I'm not a traditional person where marriage is concerned. What if I want an open relationship? What if... whatever? Those things don't fit neatly into a do-this or do-that box. I valued my therapist's professional opinion and wanted to do right by my kids. I was still carrying shame and guilt and had the sense that they'd been hard done by and were from a broken home.

So, I followed the rules the first time around. I didn't introduce the kids to the gentleman in my life until eight months into our relationship. I very much kept everything locked down. When I saw that person, I was with that person. When I was with my kids, I was with my kids. I actually had the man listed as a different name in my phone in case his name popped up and my kids saw it. Let me tell you, that was the most inauthentic thing for me. As I've said, I'm a social creature. I have a the-more-the-merrier mindset. I want all my favourite people and favourite things and favourite activities to always be coming together. I justified my inauthentic behaviour by telling myself, *If this is what it takes to protect my kids, then this is the sacrifice I have to make.* Sounds good, doesn't it? It sounds good, but it feels terrible. And anything that feels that bad and doesn't reflect the person I see when I look deep inside isn't something I can tolerate in my life for very long.

Some fish are loners, some pair up, some swim in schools. We can see that there are a lot of options out there if **we open our eyes, minds, and hearts.**

Today, I'm open with my children. I know what dating looks like for me and where my boundaries are. Now, I share my true thoughts and feelings with my children. I tell them that, for me, dating is about exploring different types of human beings. I tell them that means meeting new people and spending time with them to see if we have shared interests and values. It's no different from what many of us try to model for our kids when it comes to how to choose friends. I've explained, and they understand based on their own experiences with forming relationships, that the more time I choose to spend with someone, the more I choose to invest in them. That means that we're enjoying each other and will probably continue to enjoy each other the more we get to know each other.

While exploring online dating, I interacted with many people and had the opportunity to sidebar privately with two in more serious conversation. My kids knew both the gentlemen by name and wanted to know more about them. They were curious to get to know them better. One causally stopped by to hang out one day while we were enjoying a cottage beach day. Does that mean that they were sleeping in my bed? No. Nobody but me is waking up in my home with my kids. That's a boundary I've established. But we can all hang out together when we want to. I hang out with my girlfriends around my kids, so why is it a big deal if I hang out with friends who happen to be men when my kids are around? We've got some silly puritanical notions that are hard to shake, but it's amazing how relaxed we feel once we do. The less of a deal we make of dating, the less of a deal it is to our kids.

My kids care that I'm happy. Unfortunately, society's view that people aren't whole until they're coupled has permeated even their little brains. They worry less about me when I'm in a romantic relationship or when I have a person to hang out with. As much as I'm trying to model greatness and independence and so on, they're still a part of a world that values monogamous partnership. So, they see it as a great thing that I'm happy and enjoying other people's company. And it is a great thing. I just don't want it to be the only thing or a thing I overemphasize.

I think this relaxed mindset is good for our romantic partner(s) too. Think about how much pressure people must feel when they hear, "It's time for you to meet my kids." It's understandable that they might feel like they're being asked to take on some greater responsibility in the relationship. You want to kill dating and the lust and passion and romance in a budding relationship? Do that. Bring your new partner into a rigid situation or even give them the whiff that suddenly they're part of this ready-made family. The relaxed mindset takes the weirdness out of things for all involved. "By the way, my kids have a dad. I'm not looking for another parent for them." What I am looking for is a partner who chooses me every day and who wants to be a part of my whole life, including my family and friends.

Even though my kids want to see me happy and enjoy seeing me with someone and love getting to know the people in my life, they actually don't give a shit when a person exits because, guess what? It's not their dad leaving. It was a different thing when their dad left because he's their dad. Well, they've still got their dad. It's just that he doesn't live with their mom anymore. This new person is just Mommy's friend. Mommy's friends coming and going doesn't really impact them—this is something I've come to realize. At first, I put a lot of pressure on what an individual was going to mean to my children. Turns out, not much. Maybe that will change as they get older or as I spend more and more time with the same person. Who knows. It'll be whatever it's going to be.

Sexless, Open, and Other Relationship Arrangements

When I look back on my marriage and its final days, I can feel the pressure and shame I felt then. I wanted a husband. I wanted *my* husband. I wanted an option other than starting over at forty. I begged for him to keep our marriage intact and tried to negotiate any scenario I saw as a means to that end. I offered hall passes. We discussed having an open marriage. We'd have a "modern relationship," I told myself.

I am one hundred percent convinced that *relationship* is in most people's minds too narrowly defined. We've witnessed in our lifetime the expansion of the traditional idea of "one man, one woman" to include same-sex couples, and more and more straight cis-gender people are taking instruction from the queer community to reframe their ideas of what healthy, happy relationships can be. This also extends to non-sexual relationships. As I mentioned earlier, some marriages and co-habitation arrangements are financial arrangements. And why can't two friends choose to be life-long companions?

Some divorces are brought about by one partner awakening to their authentic sexual self or finally having the courage and freedom to embrace themselves and state their needs. For others, it's an opportunity to explore options beyond what they may have previously recognized. The point of all of it is to embody our values, understand our needs, speak our truth, and live our best lives.

We've all had someone try to comfort us with "Don't worry. There are plenty of fish in the sea." But you and I both know that most of the time they mean plenty of fish to pick one from. The thing is, some fish are loners, some pair up, some swim in schools. We can see that there are a lot of options out there if we open our eyes, minds, and hearts.

Knowing our values and having a vision for our life helps us triangulate whether we need a partner or not, and if by *partner* we mean a hot body for a one-night stand or a long-term friend, confidant, and lover, or any combination of that.

We can have wonderful lives in or out of a marriage, and there are plenty of other people who share our values and have similar lists of needs and wants. Even if one person doesn't tick all the boxes, we can find other ways to get those needs and wants met. Maybe you decide to couple up in or outside of a legal marriage arrangement and fulfill your desire to travel or dance or eat at 5-star restaurants with friends. Maybe you have an open marriage. Maybe you sleep in separate bedrooms. Maybe. Maybe. Maybe.

If you're living according to your values and all parties are consenting adults, who cares what label the thing has or if it's what your best friend, brother, or neighbour would choose. They aren't you. When we open our hearts and minds and finally accept ourselves and take responsibility for our lives, our creativity and warmth blossom. Solutions to problems others find insurmountable pop up quickly and easily. Life gets good.

All we must do is the work. We must have the courage and confidence to clearly communicate. We must be willing to have tough conversations and not bend to the wishes and will of those around us. We thrive when we do the work, and we create opportunities to model greatness for our children. How great is it that we get a second, third, fourth, and so on chance to show them healthy lifestyle choices and what relationships and intimacy actually looks like? How great is it that we can include them in this process?

All Relationships Change

No matter how much we may want it to be otherwise, the reality is that the hot and heavy part of a relationship fades, especially when people live together. We start talking about the furnace being on the fritz and how much it's going to cost to fix it, about who's driving who where and when. Sexting will be replaced with requests to pick up bread, and whispers of sweet nothings in the middle of the night will be replaced by shoulder nudges and "You're snoring again."

It ain't the glamour life. It's better. It's endearing, boring, beautiful, and oh so freeing as long as we get there in the healthiest way possible and as long as we're living our life according to how we want to live it, not by some other person's or group's definition of right and reasonable.

If there is a silver lining to the pain and self-doubt I experienced early on, it's that I wasn't in a hurry to jump back into the ocean, a pond, or even a puddle. I don't give all the same advice my therapist gave me, but I agree with her when she says not to be in a hurry. To that I add manage your expectations, date yourself first, kiss a lot of frogs, and have fun. And I'm convinced that if someone shows up in our lives, they've shown up for good reason. I truly believe that every single person who comes into our lives is there to teach us something.

Conclusion
Show Up to Play Big

THERE IS no one-size-fits-all in life or in love. Maybe that's why they call books like this "self-help," because you get to explore ideas and experiment without any outside pressure and undue influence. You get to choose your destination, set your course, and stop as often as you like to rest or take in the views. You get to walk, pedal, wheel, or drive, and you get to determine how far and how fast you go. The road ahead is yours to take, but there are some hazards. These hazards are mostly of the mind.

It's easy to slip into the old habit of comparing ourselves to those around us, particularly those who've walked this road before. You may look at me, in fact, and think that you'll never stack up. You may think that you're never going to get where I am. You absolutely can, but I made sacrifices to get here. I practiced deliberate decision making that involved unpacking my backpack and leaving thoughts and people that were weighing me down and who wouldn't appreciate the destination even if I carried them along. Day in and day out, whether I wanted to or not, I did the hard things. I worked the mental and emotional muscles needed to move me forward. I took one hundred percent responsibility for my life.

No matter how beautiful and pleasant the destination is, you won't get there if you don't move toward it. And you straight up won't get there if you don't do the work. This is hard stuff. Your divorce may drag on for years. It may take years to find common ground with your former partner and anyone else your children tie you to that you would otherwise choose to cut loose. If you've gotta carry that burden, lighten your load in other ways. And I encourage you to look not just at the outcome of women who are ahead of you. Remember what we went through and take comfort in the fact that, if you're facing it, somebody out there has already gone through it. You can too.

Show up every day. Embrace that abundance mindset. Shed the expectations and stigmas that have limited you your entire life. And take at least one step toward confidence every single day.

We're not talking about a dating or dieting mindset. We don't just hop on and off this bandwagon. We're *living*—present tense, active voice—our best life. We understand that we're not moving to distract ourselves from pain or to simply look busy. With every step we take, no matter how small, we're building momentum that propels us closer to our authentic selves and the confidence we've been missing.

I still was in a very negative space with my former partner when we finally signed the divorce papers. I was friendly, but we were not friends. It took about three more years before I finally crossed the border between what was past and the vision I had for my new life. Lee and I can now talk openly about our relationship. We co-parent, and through that we've developed a friendship and the ability to sit at holiday tables together. That may never happen for many of you. It takes

*Now is the time
to dream, and*
dream big.

two people to marry, it takes two people to divorce, and it takes two people to be friends. My relationship with my former partner isn't perfect, but it's better than I ever expected.

Learning to accept my imperfections and evaluate my actions according to my best intentions has helped me show the same openness to others. I'm still learning to drive this car, though, and sometimes I face headwinds and hit patches of black ice. On really bad days, I skid off onto the shoulder of the road. That's okay. I know where I'm going. I put my foot back on the gas and reorient as needed. If I'm stuck well and good, I flag down a fellow traveller to help me get back on the road. I know that I'll never actually reach my destination because as soon as I get to the spot on my map, I'll see further ahead. New adventures will beckon, and new roads will appear. I don't need all the answers. I don't even need to know where I'll get the energy. I'm the leading lady. I'm the Mother. Fucking. Mom. I know that when I decide to go somewhere and do something, it's going to happen. I know that the people and fuel I need will appear along the way. All I have to do is keep on moving and keep my heart and eyes wide open.

Before your it's-over moment, had you given up on your dreams? Did you have a written bucket list? Maybe you had a vague sense of what you wanted to do in the future but not enough hope to commit it to paper. Now is the time to dream, and dream big. This is not an end but a beginning!

Those of us who weren't living the dream or whose dreams were shattered have a new lease on life. And we're older, we're wiser, we have less filter. Those of us in our forties or fifties also know that we've got a shorter runway to work with, so time is of the essence. This is empowering! We have a sense of excited urgency.

Regardless of how old we are, we finally know who we are, what we want, and what's standing in our way. Pressure to bake cookies for the school bake sale? Forget that shit. If you don't want to, you don't have to. People's judgement? So what. Who are they and what do they know? Living to serve others so they can climb mountains, sail across oceans, and do good in the world? Only if I want to.

What if we flipped the script and redefined the bucket list? What if, instead of listing all the things we want to do before we kick the bucket, our bucket list was about all the people, things, and experiences that could fill our bucket? What if we lived every day in a way that filled that bucket of thirst-quenching life to overflowing, allowing us to share our life-giving authentic selves with our children, our friends, our relatives, and every stranger who looked to us in admiration and with hope because they see that if we can do it, they too can hit the do-over button?

If there's one thing life has taught us, it's that fairy tales are just that, tales—untrue narratives meant to entertain and even control us. But we know better now. We've experienced reality. It's bittersweet to be sure, but it's *freedom*. If you take anything away from this book, I hope it's this: You have the power to change your story and thrive through divorce and beyond with grit and grace.

Acknowledgements

FIRST AND FOREMOST, my deepest gratitude for my friends and family, who never ever, not even for one second, surprised me. You shared space, held me up, pushed me through, and always made me laugh even when it seemed more like a crying kinda moment.

To my family, who have witnessed a little girl with big dreams fall and stumble and climb to the top again—you stand for nothing less than my source of empowerment. Thank you for always being my first call, my first flight out, and my guiding light, knowing and loving all of me.

Mom and Dad, my first call—thank you for holding space no matter when and no matter what. Words cannot express the feeling of coming home with heavy news. You held me in my familiar nest, reminded me I could fly, and championed my vision for my new family while honouring Lee, Ava, and Giacomo as if nothing had changed—because in your hearts nothing had.

Greg, my baby bro, my first flight out—I will never forget landing to your open arms, where I felt as home as I ever had since my journey through uncoupling began. Our eight-hour walk, pounding the pavement until our souls settled safely, grounded me to my core. Time stood still as we reflected, laughed, and cried; as always you received me unconditionally. Thank you for being my person who raised my first vibration for hope when I did not know how to move forward yet.

To my children, Ava and Giacomo: watching you grow, walking alongside you, and losing track of time in every snuggle is my greatest honour and happiest joy. I love you with all my heart and soul. Thank you for exploring, nurturing, and creating every adventure, tradition, and milestone that is us, our family, our way—you both inspire me to try harder, go further, love more, and worry less because in you I see me and in me I see you, and very simply put all that matters are the stolen moments we share in our time together!

To Carm and Fil, the greatest in-laws a gal could ever imagine—we've travelled many roads with many destinations, but this journey you didn't have to travel, you chose to. Your unconditional love, friendship, and support never skipped a beat and to this day is a beautiful connection that I will forever treasure.

And to my friends, who are nothing short of my miracle during the eye of a storm. To my dream team and ultimately my golden girls—from dancing on tables to dancing on bars, from dinner debates and oceanside loungers, there is nothing we can't solve because life is just better together. To my Miami girls: you are my rock, a beautiful gift to my journey who always make me feel loved, supported, and seen through every milestone; with you I can strategize with red, rosé, sparkling, and miles of shopping racks, with #faster sometimes all that needs to be said.

To my partner in crime through divorce: our friendship is life-long, so clearly we know how to choose a good thing when we see it. Thank you for always checking in, crushing firsts, flirting with disaster, and dreaming about the future because we have not come this far only to come this far.

To my Jacobson crew, who group-hugged me so tight I couldn't help but surrender to the process, feeling safely supported. To my forum girls, old and new, who hold space and time in the bubble while the real world spins around. To my only friend who can have me first-date-night ready with wax strips between the cheeks. To my garden ciggies, boat cruises, and friends I'd like to date (yes, in a sorta romantic way and with all the benefits): your wisdom, fun, and get-up-and-go keep me out of my head. To my divide and conquer, who lifted me up and held my children when I could not—grateful is an understatement, but words cannot do justice. To my divorced trailblazing friends, who helped to give me hope and perspective, and who taught me the importance of taking my "one" shot and doing this right—like the Mother Fucking Mom I am. To my Crocodile Dundee, who showed me that dating after marriage can be safe, sacred, and beautiful. To my true ride or die, who holds my heart, my hand, and my melody in a way that allows me to dance like no one is watching—I love you and all the ways you show up to love and be loved. You are all my source of inspiration, fortitude, and hearty belly laughs—my inner circle that is my beating heart!

To my besties' hubbies, because in all the divine feminine energy that surrounded me with TLC, the balance of your masculine energy and firm but gentle support helped me find power in the everyday with a play-to-win mindset while navigating my new independence—from dinner parties to power tools to calling me back to the driver's seat, you had my back.

To my therapist, Dr. Karyn Gordon, who kept me safely moving through my pain at my rock bottom and who gently showed me how to rebuild myself. For giving my kids their mom during dark days and an even brighter future.

To Gabby Bernstein, for being my turning point and a beacon in my storm, and for lighting my purpose on fire with your books and your bestsellers masterclass. You made this book possible.

To Cristen Iris, who kicked the book over the goal line. It was a true pleasure writing with you. Your ability to streamline, unpack, and create story is impeccable. For me, for what is so emotional, raw, and too close to be fairly objective, you brilliantly bridged the gap so that our reader can have the best experience and a-ha moments one chapter at a time.

To Page Two, who believed in my mission to eliminate the stigma of divorce so much that it became a reality. Jesse, Amanda, Taysia, Melissa, Meghan, Rony, and the entire team: You are the final leg of this journey, and you have embraced a professional spirit of publishing work ethic and integrity as much as you have been my cheerleaders with a cause— we did it!

To Darius and Kelly, because creating the cover was as much fun as it looks: You are brilliant to be able to combine a rigour and creativity that makes it all look so effortless!

To my magician, Leanne Webb, who saw the possibility for this book to be not only a mission but an incredible resource that could impact millions of women to thrive through divorce and life beyond. Lemonade Life, Unwife, and all things Squeeze related exist because two women believed they could do more with less and have a shit-ton of fun for life along the way!

To the Lemonade Life Ladies: Leanne, Rafaa, Amanda, Laura, Deborah, Suzanne, Katie, and so many more—for catching and throwing the lemons out in front and behind the scenes every day.

Last but certainly not least, to Lee, for without you this book would not be possible. Not for the obvious reason, but for all the beauty that is my journey. My journey will forever be connected to our journey. You are a man of integrity, a leader among leaders, and one of my favourite humans. I am forever grateful for our journey as friends, husband and wife, and co-parents. I could not think of a better partner to navigate life in a way that honours us being the true makers of our own destiny. Thank you for having courage, for speaking truth, and for daring greatly, but mostly for being my first love story and the daddy to our most beautiful children—our family, our way!

More Resources

Personality & Job Aptitude Tests

- 16 Personalities: *16personalities.com*
- Monster.com top 10 career tests: *monster.com/ career-advice/article/best-free-career-assessment-tools*

Information on Narcissism/Co-dependency

- Dr. Raman Durvasula YouTube channel: *youtube.com/user/doctorramandurvasula*
- *The Human Magnet Syndrome* by Ross Rosenberg
- Richard Grannon (a.k.a. The Spartan Life Coach) YouTube channel: *youtube.com/c/richardgrannon*

Let's Make Lemonade!

HERE IS a snapshot of the resources you will find at **LemonadeLife.ca**:

- Checklists, Guides, and Planners for everything you need to know to navigate separation and divorce

- Blogs and Articles on anything and everything related to divorce—from telling your kids to reclaiming your bedroom and everything in between!

- Quotes, Affirmations, and all the Inspiration you need to get through the toughest of days

- Unwife—my flagship program that supports you through the process of separation and divorce from start to finish. I'll personally be there with you every step of the way—as your friend, confidant, coach, and accountability partner

Reach out at **connect@lemonadelife.ca**

⊙ @lemonadelifecoach
❶ @thelemonadelifecoach
🐦 @lemonadecoach #lemonadelife #unwife
Ⓟ @lemonadelifecoach

The Bucket List Challenge

BEFORE YOU GO...
Thank you so much for sharing your time and energy with me and for allowing me to walk alongside you on this leg of your journey.

If you've found value in this book, please help me spread this message to other women like us by leaving an honest review on your online retailer of choice.

Thank you in advance for your consideration and effort and for walking this road with me.

ALICIA

DARIUS BASHAR

About the Author

ALICIA ROBERTSON is passionate about helping women divorce with confidence. She is a certified life coach, founder of Lemonade Life, and creator of Unwife, a flagship program that teaches women to thrive through divorce. Trained in mindfulness, positive psychology, and neuroscience, Alicia helps women navigate divorce with grit and grace, become confident and informed decision makers, and create their best life.

In addition to this work, Alicia is also a social media authority with a weekly newsletter and community called *The Squeeze*. She has been featured on Family Talk Radio, *Women on Topp*, and Thrive Global.

Alicia lives in Ontario, Canada, with her two young children and dog, Mac.

LemonadeLife.ca

CPSIA information can be obtained
at www.ICGtesting.com
Printed in the USA
BVHW071434010422
632670BV00002B/9